101

WINNING FOOTBALL DRILLS

From the Legends of the Game

Jerry Tolley

ISBN: 1-58518-731-3
Library of Congress Control Number: 2002113532
Book layout and diagrams: Deborah Oldenburg
Cover design: Kerry Hartjen
Front cover photo: Allsport

Coaches Choice
P.O. Box 1828
Monterey, CA 93942
www.coacheschoice.com

Charlie McClendon
1923-2001

Charlie "Cholly Mac" McClendon began his legendary coaching career under Bear Bryant in 1950 at the University of Kentucky. Three years later he came to Louisiana State University and as an assistant coach helped lead the Tigers to the 1958 national championship. He was elevated to head coach after the 1961 season.

Charlie served 18 years as head coach at LSU, becoming the Tigers' most successful coach by achieving an overall record of 137-59-7. During his LSU tenure, he garnered 16 winning seasons. He coached 21 first-team All-Americans and 56 players who earned All-SEC honors.

Charlie was named SEC Coach of the Year in 1969 and 1970, and he was voted National Coach of the Year in 1970 after leading his Tigers to a 9-3 record. Eleven of his teams won eight or more games.

After Leaving LSU, Charlie spent two years as the Executive Director of the Tangerine Bowl (now the Florida Citrus Bowl). In 1982 he became the Executive Director of the American Football Coaches Association. He served the AFCA, with distinction, for 12 years before his retirement in 1994. In recent years he administered a scholarship fund to provide scholarship aid to the children of former LSU football players.

A native of Lewisville, Arkansas, Charlie was inducted into the National Football Foundation's College Hall of Fame in 1986, and in 1992 he received the Amos Alonzo Stagg Award for his outstanding "service in the advancement of the best interest of football."

Sharing in his success throughout his career was his wife of 54 years, Dorothy Faye, who has been described as "the classiest, most elegant and ageless coaching wife in Southeastern Conference history." Charlie once remarked that he could never understand why the prettiest girl at Arkansas A&M would marry an "ugly ol' cuss" like him.

Charlie McClendon represented the very best of what a football coach should be. His dedication and love for the game, his players and his assistant coaches were admired and respected by everyone who knew him. Charlie will be remembered as one the most beloved figures in the history of the LSU football program. He will be missed.

Glenn "Bo" Schembechler
Former Head Football Coach
University of Michigan

ACKNOWLEDGMENTS

Sincere appreciation is expressed to the 101 football-coaching legends who have contributed to this book. Their commitment to the time-honored tradition of the sharing of ideas among the coaching fraternity made the editorship of this publication both an honor and a privilege.*

Gratitude is also expressed to Kristin Simonetti, a student at Elon University, and my sons, Jay and Justin Tolley, for their editorial assistance and masterful job of typing the manuscript. Also thanked is Heather Goggans, Development Communications Officer at Elon, for proofing the text, and Jimma Causey for her administrative support. Mr. Kyle Wills, a friend and Associate Athletics Director at Elon, is acknowledged for the illustrations accompanying each drill.

A loving appreciation is expressed to my wonderful wife, Joanie, for her patience, understanding, and support.

* Special appreciation is extended to each of the contributing coaches who verified that all compiled biographical information was accurate. It should be noted that all information, including win-loss statistics and individual honors, reflects only that which had occurred before May 31, 2002.

FOREWORD

Jerry Tolley, a former National Coach of the Year, won back-to-back national titles at Elon University in 1980 and 1981. In this exceptional book, 101 Winning Football Drills from the Legends of the Game, Dr. Tolley has compiled the ultimate drill book for football coaches.

This unprecedented practical guidebook contains drills fundamental to every football position, in addition to drills specifically related to passing, option play, tackling, agility, defensive pursuit, combination and team play, cardiovascular endurance, and all phases of the kicking game. Jerry presents each drill complete with the objective of the drill, the equipment it requires, the exact description of each drill, explicit coaching points, safety considerations, illustrations, and drill variations. Specific safety factors are highlighted with each drill. The appendices of this book also include essential information concerning relevant medical and legal considerations, as well as comprehensive guidelines designed to help coaches better prepare athletes for the grueling conditions of two-a-day workouts.

The 101 coaching legends featured in this one-of-a-kind publication collectively have compiled a 18,373-8,403-508 win-loss record*, representing over 2,300 seasons of coaching excellence at every level of collegiate play. Their teams have captured 158 national titles, and individually have been selected national coach of the year by a variety of selecting bodies160 times. Thirty have served as presidents of the American Football Coaches Association, while 18 have been awarded the Amos Alonzo Stagg award for their outstanding service in the advancement of the best interest of football. Thirty-seven have been enshrined in the College Football Hall of Fame. This comprehensive drill book is one of legendary dimensions.

Dr. Tom Osborne
Former Head Football Coach
University of Nebraska

* As of May 31, 2002

CONTENTS

PART I
OFFENSIVE DRILLS

CHAPTER 1

Running Back

Drills

DRILL #1: BAG DRILL

John H. McKay (Deceased)
University of Southern California, Tampa Bay Buccaneers
Overall Record: 171-128-9
National Champions: 1962, 1967, 1972, and 1974
National Coach of the Year: 1962 and 1972
College Football Hall of Fame: 1988
AFCA President: 1973

Objective: To teach and practice the proper fundamentals and techniques of running the football. Incorporated are skills related to receiving a handoff, cutting, protecting the football, power, balance, and ball awareness.

Equipment Needed: One large blocking dummy, three hand shields, and footballs

Description:

- Position a player holding a large blocking dummy on a selected line of scrimmage. Two additional players with hand shields are placed side-by-side and five-yards behind the front dummy holder. A fourth player holding a hand shield is positioned another five-yards downfield (see diagram).

- Running backs line up in a straight line five-yards behind the large blocking dummy.

- The coach is positioned in a dive relationship to the row of running backs.

- On coach's cadence and snap count, the first running back drives from his stance and receives the handoff.

- As the runner approaches the first blocking dummy, the player holding that dummy tilts it either left or right. The ballcarrier breaks the opposite way of the tilted dummy and sprints to the defenders holding the hand shields.

- He now blasts through the hand shields as the defenders *jam* him and try to prevent his progress.

- The ballcarrier now sprints past the final shield holder as that defender throws the shield at the runner's feet. The ballcarrier executes a high step to avoid tripping or falling.

- The drill continues until all running backs have had a sufficient number of repetitions.

- The handoffs should be executed both left and right.

Coaching Points:

- Always check to see that running backs are aligned correctly and are in their proper stances.
- Instruct running backs to keep their eyes straight-ahead and focused on the blocking dummy as they receive the handoff.
- Make sure that running backs' shoulders are low and squared to the defenders as they explode through the collision area.
- Instruct runners to kick through the thrown dummy to simulate breaking a tackle.
- Insist that the drill be conducted at full speed.

Safety Considerations:

- Proper warm-up should precede the drill.
- Instruct the defenders in the collision area not to be abusive as they *jam* the ballcarrier.

Variation:

- Can be used with or without any one of the dummy or hand-shield areas.

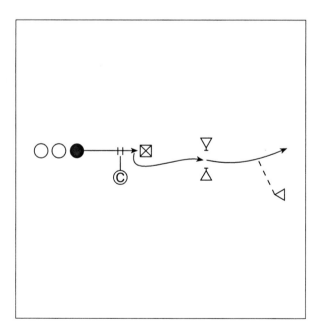

DRILL #2: BARREL RUN

Grant G. Teaff
McMurry University, Angelo State University, Baylor University
Overall Record: 170-150-8
National Coach of the Year: Baylor 1974
College Football Hall of Fame: 2001
AFCA Executive Director: 1994-present

Objective: To teach and practice the proper fundamentals and techniques of running the football. Incorporated are skills related to reading, protecting the football, quickness, reaction, balance, and explosion.

Equipment Needed: Five large barrels, three large blocking dummies, and footballs

Description:

- Place five barrels two-feet apart as shown in the diagram.
- Position two defenders behind the back two barrels with instructions to grab for the football as a ballcarrier comes by.
- Place three large blocking dummies with a holder in a triangular alignment three-yards behind the barrel area. Two yards separate the three dummies.
- Align a row of ballcarriers five yards in front of the drill area.
- The coach is positioned behind the middle barrel.
- On command, the first ballcarrier drives from his stance and sprints between the first two barrels as the coach appears from behind either side of the middle barrel.
- The ballcarrier now cuts in the opposite direction and moves up and around the middle barrel.
- As the runner sprints between the back two barrels, the defenders positioned behind them reach out and try to pull the football away from the ballcarrier.
- The running back now drives into the middle standup dummy and spins out either left or right. He then cuts off the back dummy according to the way the dummy is tilted by the holder.
- The drill continues until all the running backs have had a sufficient number of repetitions.

Coaching Points:

- Always check to see that the running backs are aligned correctly and are in their proper stances.
- Always stress the importance of carrying the football properly.
- Instruct the running backs to use a lateral step when breaking away from the movement of the coach from behind the middle barrel.
- Insist that all running backs keep their heads up throughout the entire drill.
- Insist that the drill be conducted at full speed.

Safety Considerations:

- Proper warm-up should precede the drill.
- Helmets should always be worn with chinstraps snapped.
- Check barrels regularly to make sure they are free of sharp edges.

Variation:

- Can be used with various dummy alignments and running back movements in finishing the drill.

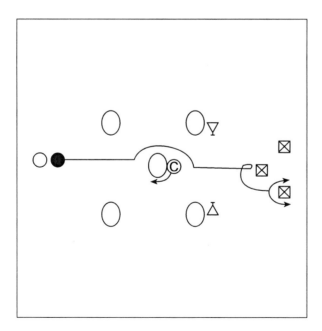

DRILL #3: BLAST DRILL

Robert "Bob" Devaney (Deceased)
University of Wyoming, University of Nebraska
Overall Record: 136-30-7
National Champions: Nebraska 1970 and 1971
National Coach of the Year: Nebraska 1971
College Football Hall of Fame: 1981
Amos Alonzo Stagg Award: 1994

Objective: To teach and practice the proper fundamentals and techniques of running the football. Incorporated are skills related to receiving a handoff, tackle avoidance, balance, and carrying and protecting the football.

Equipment Needed: Three large blocking dummies and footballs

Description:

- Position two players holding large blocking dummies one-yard apart on a selected line of scrimmage. A third dummy is held three-yards behind the players holding the front two dummies.

- A quarterback is aligned one yard in front of either of the two front-held dummies and in a dive relationship to a row of running backs. (See diagram)

- On the quarterback's cadence and snap count, the first running back drives from his stance and receives the handoff.

- He now *blasts* through the collision area as the two dummy holders *jam* him and try to prevent his progress.

- The ballcarrier continues his run and drives into the third dummy and then spins off either left or right and sprints for a designated distance.

- The drill continues until all running backs have had a sufficient number of repetitions.

- The handoffs should be executed both left and right.

Coaching Points:

- Always check to see that running backs are aligned correctly and are in their proper stances.

- Instruct the running backs to focus their eyes straight ahead as they receive the handoff.

- Insist that the drill be conducted at full speed.

Safety Considerations:

- Proper warm-up should precede the drill.
- Instruct the defenders in the collision area not to be too aggressive as they *jam* the ballcarrier.

Variation:

- Can be used with various running-back movements in attacking the final dummy (stiff arm, sidestep, etc.).

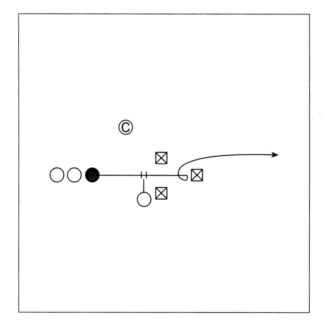

DRILL #4: CADENCE AND HANDOFF

Dave Maurer
Wittenberg University
Overall Record: 129-23-3
National Champions: 1973 and 1975
National Coach of the Year: 1973 and 1975
College Football Hall of Fame: 1991
AFCA President: 1984

Objective: To teach and practice the proper fundamentals and techniques in executing the handoff. Special emphasis is placed on cadence recognition.

Equipment Needed: Eight large blocking dummies and footballs

Description:

- Lay two rows of four blocking dummies seven-feet apart. A three-yard separation is between each dummy (see diagram).
- Position a quarterback holding a football one-yard back and to the outside of the first dummy on each side.
- Align a row of running backs behind each row of dummies and in a dive relationship to the quarterback.
- The coach stands at the end of, and in between, the two rows of dummies. He designates different quarterbacks to call cadence.
- On designated quarterback's cadence and snap count, both quarterbacks execute the dive handoffs to their respective running back.
- After receiving the handoff, the running backs run over and through the dummies. Running backs are instructed to change lines after each repetition.
- The drill continues until all drill participants have had a sufficient number of repetitions.

Coaching Points:

- Check to see that all personnel are aligned correctly and are in their proper stances.
- Instruct the quarterbacks to call their cadence with authority.
- Make sure that quarterback *feathers* the football on the running back's *belt buckle* and that he rides the ballcarrier after the ball exchange has been executed.
- Instruct running backs to anticipate the snap count, form good pockets for receiving the football, and focus their eyes straight ahead.

Safety Considerations:

- Proper warm-up should precede the drill.
- Helmets should be worn with chinstraps snapped.

Variations:

- Can incorporate centers.
- Can be used with coach flashing fingers and with running backs calling out the correct numbers to ensure that ballcarriers are focusing on the point of attack.

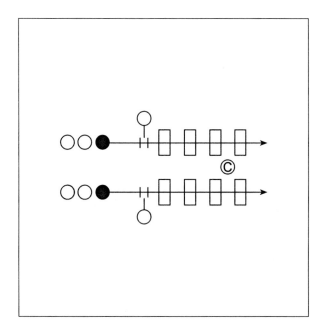

DRILL #5: FIGURE-EIGHT DRILL OR MONKEY ROLL

Richard "Dick" Tomey
University of Hawaii, University of Arizona
Overall Record: 158-110-4

Objective: To teach and practice the proper fundamentals of holding on to the football.

Equipment Needed: Three footballs

Description:

- Position three running backs, each holding a football, two-yards apart on a selected line of scrimmage. Other running backs fall in behind the first three drill participants.
- The coach stands in front of the three lines.
- On the coach's first command, the first three running backs step forward five yards and assume the *football position*. On coach's second command, the drill participants execute the standard figure-eight *monkey roll* as follows:
  - The middle running back hits the ground rolling to his right.
  - The running back positioned to the right of the middle running back dives sideways over the middle running back and rolls to his left.
  - The third running back dives over the second running back and rolls to his right.
  - This procedure continues for seven to eight seconds.
- On the coach's third command, the three running backs stand in place *chopping* their feet.
- On the coach's final command, the three running backs sprint up the field for ten yards.
- The drill continues until all running backs have had a sufficient number of repetitions.
- The drill should be conducted both left and right and with the football tucked under each arm.

Coaching Points:

- Insist that all running backs secure the football properly.
- Instruct all running backs to regain their feet after each roll.
- Insist that the drill be conducted at full speed.

Safety Considerations:

- Proper warm-up should precede the drill.
- The drill should progress from half speed to full speed.

Variation:

- Can be used for all ball-handling positions.

DRILL #6: FULLBACK-SWEEP BLOCK

Terry M. Donahue
University of California at Los Angeles
Overall Record: 151-74-8
College Football Hall of Fame: 2000

Objective: To teach and practice the proper fundamentals and techniques in the execution of the fullback's block on the sweep play. This block may vary according to the play of the defense, and the fullback must be able to adjust his block as the play develops.

Equipment Needed: Three cones, one hand shield, and footballs

Description:

- Align a center, quarterback, fullback, and running back over the football on a selected line of scrimmage.

- Position three cones three-yards apart and perpendicular to the line of scrimmage across from the offensive tackle position. These cones define the inside boundary of the sweep.

- A defender holding a hand shield is aligned anywhere between the inside linebacker and outside rolled-up cornerback positions. He is instructed to stop the sweep play from any position, from any angle, and with varying degrees of penetration across the line of scrimmage.

- On quarterback cadence and ball snap, the offense executes the *toss* sweep with the fullback adjusting his block according to the way the defender plays.

- The drill continues until all drill participants have had a sufficient number of repetitions.

- The drill should be conducted both left and right and from various field positions.

Coaching Points:

- Always check to see that all personnel are aligned correctly and are in their proper stances.

- Instruct the fullbacks to take an angle toward the defender that will make it impossible for the defender to move under their blocks without allowing the ballcarriers to go to the outside, or move around the fullbacks without giving the ballcarrier a lane to the inside.

- Instruct the ballcarrier always to stay behind and stay deeper than the fullback.

- To block an inside linebacker penetrating to the inside, the fullbacks should execute a shoulder block. To block a cornerback penetrating to the outside, the fullbacks should use a reverse-body block. A rolling-body block should be used against an outside penetrator who plays with a low, hard shoulder pad.

Safety Considerations:

- Proper warm-up should precede the drill.
- The drill area should be clear of all foreign articles.
- The drill should progress from walk-through to full speed.
- The coach should monitor closely the intensity of the drill.
- Instruct all fullbacks as to the proper fundamentals and techniques of the various blocks to be executed.

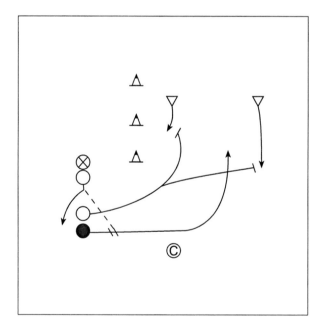

DRILL #7: HIGH KNEE–HANG ON–HIT

Ben Schwartzwalder (Deceased)
High School, Muhlenberg College, Syracuse University
Overall Record: 178-96-3
National Champions: Syracuse 1959
National Coach of the Year: Syracuse 1959
College Football Hall of Fame: 1982
Amos Alonzo Stagg Award: 1977
AFCA President: 1967

Objective: To teach and practice the proper fundamentals and techniques of running and securing the football, with a special emphasis on high knee action, leg drive, and power.

Equipment Needed: Three large blocking dummies, two hand shields, and footballs

Description:

- Lay three large blocking dummies one-yard apart and parallel to each other (see diagram).
- Align two rows of linemen just behind dummy area. Two yards separate the two rows of linemen.
- Two additional linemen holding hand shields are positioned behind the two rows of linemen.
- Position a row of running backs five yards in front of the first blocking dummy.
- On the coach's command, the first running back sprints over the dummies and then runs through the gauntlet of linemen as they try to jerk the football from his hands.
- After clearing the gauntlet, the running back lowers his shoulders and explodes through the defenders holding the hand shields as they try to impede his progress.
- The drill continues until all running backs have had a sufficient number of repetitions.

Coaching Points:

- Emphasize the importance of a quick start and high-knee lifts through the dummy area.
- Emphasize the importance of securing the football through the gauntlet and collision areas.

- Instruct the running backs to lower their center of gravity as they explode through the collision area.

Safety Considerations:

- It is imperative that proper warm-up precede the drill.
- Instruct the linemen in the collision area not to be abusive as they *jam* the running backs.

Variation:

- Can be used as a tight end and wide receiver drill.

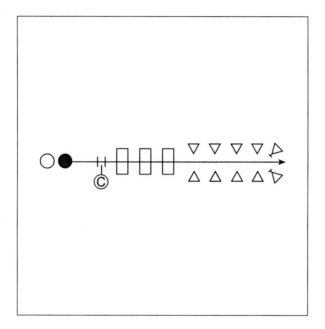

DRILL #8: RUNNING-PASS DRILL

Don B. Faurot (Deceased)
Truman State University, University of Missouri
Overall Record: 163-93-13
College Football Hall of Fame: 1961
Amos Alonzo Stagg Award: 1964
AFCA President: 1953

Objective: To teach and practice the proper fundamentals and techniques in the execution of the halfback pass off the option play.

Equipment Needed: Footballs

Description:

- Align an offense (center, quarterback, running back, and wide receiver) over the football on a selected line of scrimmage.
- Position a cornerback in his regular alignment over the wide receiver.
- Other drill participants stand adjacent to their drill area.
- On quarterback's cadence and ball snap, the offense executes the halfback-option pass as the running back keys the cornerback.
- If cornerback attacks line of scrimmage, running back passes the football to wide receiver on a flag pattern. If cornerback covers receiver, running back tucks football away and sprints downfield.
- The drill continues until all drill participants have had a sufficient number of repetitions.
- The drill should be conducted both left and right and from various positions on the field.

Coaching Points:

- Always check to see that all personnel are aligned correctly and are in their proper stances.
- Instruct the running backs to key the cornerback and to make the play look like an option run.
- Make sure all running backs practice the proper mechanics in throwing all passes.

Safety Considerations:

- Proper warm-up should precede the drill.
- The drill area should be clear of all foreign articles. This includes the sideline areas.
- This is not recommended as a contact drill.

Variations:

- Can incorporate a tight end.
- Can be used from various formations.
- Can be used as a wide-receiver drill.
- Can be used as a defensive-back drill.

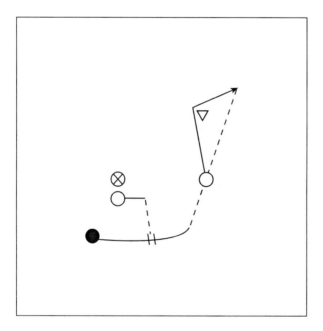

DRILL #9: SIDELINE DRILL

J. Frank Broyles
University of Missouri, University of Arkansas
Overall Record: 142-62-6
National Champions: Arkansas 1964
National Coach of the Year: Arkansas 1964
College Football Hall of Fame: 1983
AFCA President: 1970

Objective: To teach and practice the proper fundamentals and techniques of running the football with special emphasis on staying in bounds.

Equipment Needed: Three hand shields and footballs

Description:

- Align an offense (center, quarterback, and running back) over the football on the left-hash mark of a selected line of scrimmage.
- Position three defenders, holding hand shields, four-yards apart and three yards from the near sideline. The first shield holder stands on the line of scrimmage.
- Other drill participants stand adjacent to the drill area.
- On quarterback's cadence and ball snap, the first running back drives from his stance, takes the pitch, sprints to the sideline, and cuts upfield. He then runs past the three shield holders as they try to force him out of bounds.
- The drill continues until all running backs have had a sufficient number of repetitions.
- The drill should be conducted from both the left and right hash marks.

Coaching Points:

- Always check to see that all personnel are aligned correctly and are in their proper stances.
- Insist that all running backs carry the football under the outside arm.
- Instruct the running backs to lower their shoulders and to drive into each shield holder with an inside forearm-shoulder blow.
- Insist that the drill be conducted at full speed.

Safety Considerations:

- Proper warm-up should precede the drill.
- The drill area should be clear of all foreign articles. This includes the sideline areas.
- Instruct shield holders not to abuse the running backs and never *jam* them in the head area.

Variations:

- Can be used with a varying number of shield holders.
- Can be used with different backfield actions.
- Can be used as a center-quarterback ball-exchange drill.

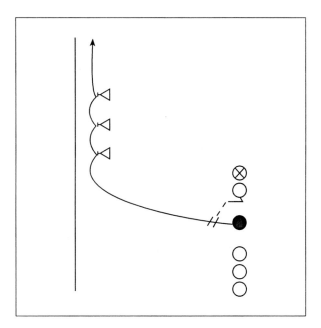

DRILL #10: TIRE DRILL

James "Jim" Wacker
Texas Lutheran University, North Dakota State University, Southwest Texas
State University, Texas Christian University, University of Minnesota
Overall Record: 160-130-3
National Champions: Texas Lutheran 1974 and 1975;
Southwest Texas State 1981 and 1982
National Coach of the Year: Southwest Texas 1982; Texas Christian 1984

Objective: To teach and practice the proper fundamentals and techniques of running the football. Incorporated are skills related to reading, reacting, and acceleration.

Equipment Needed: 20 car tires, three blocking dummies, and footballs

Description:

- Position five stacks of tires (four high) as shown in the diagram. The distance between the stacks of tires varies according to the skill level of the running backs.

- Place three blocking dummies in a row and parallel to the back two stacks of tires. Two yards separate each of the three dummies.

- Position a quarterback, holding a football, in a dive relationship to a row of running backs in front of the tires.

- The coach or manager stands behind the middle stack of tires.

- On quarterback's cadence and snap count, the first running back drives from his stance and receives the handoff. He runs between the first two stacks of tires as the coach appears from behind either side of the middle tires.

- The running back now cuts in the opposite direction. He then moves up and around the middle tires and between the back two stacks of tires.

- Now the running back accelerates over and through the three blocking dummies.

- The drill continues until all running backs have had a sufficient number of repetitions.

- The drill should be conducted from both left- and right-handoff alignments.

Coaching Points:

- Always check to see that the running backs are aligned correctly and are in their proper stances.

- Instruct the running backs to make as sharp a cut as possible.

- Make sure the running backs accelerate over and through the dummy area.
- Make sure that all quarterbacks carry out all fakes after executing the handoff.
- Insist that the drill be conducted at full speed.

Safety Consideration:

- Proper warm-up should precede the drill.

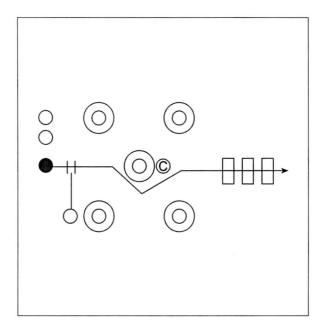

DRILL #11: WET-BALL DRILL

Fred S. Akers
University of Wyoming, University of Texas, Purdue University
Overall Record: 113-82-3
National Coach of the Year: Texas 1977

Objective: To teach and practice the proper fundamentals and techniques of receiving and running with a wet football. Incorporated are skills related to reaction, agility, and quickness.

Equipment Needed: Eight large blocking dummies, one bucket of water, and footballs

Description:

- Align two defenders holding blocking dummies one-yard apart on a selected line of scrimmage.

- Lay three blocking dummies one behind the other and one-yard behind the two defenders holding the front dummies. The blocking dummies are placed horizontal to the line of scrimmage and two yards separate each dummy. Alternating running backs are positioned on both sides of each of the three dummies, forming a gauntlet.

- Three additional dummies are held in a triangular relationship seven-yards behind the front three dummies. The coach holds the dummy forming the apex of the triangle (see diagram).

- The quarterback stands to either side of the front of the drill area and in a selected play relationship to a running back. He holds a wet football taken from a water bucket adjacent to his drill area.

- On cadence and snap count, the running back drives from his stance and receives the wet football from the quarterback. He then *blasts* through the paired dummies and sprints over and through the three dummies as the alternating running back tries to jerk the football from his hands.

- After clearing the gauntlet area, the running back sprints toward the triangle-dummy area as the coach tilts his dummy either left or right. The running back breaks in the opposite direction and runs through the back two held dummies.

- The drill continues until all running backs have had a sufficient number of repetitions.

- The drill should be conducted from both a left- and right-handoff alignment.

Coaching Points:

- Always check to see that running backs are aligned correctly and are in their proper stances.
- Emphasize the importance of body lean, good leg action, and securing the football throughout the drill.
- Insist that the drill be conducted at full speed.

Safety Considerations:

- Proper warm-up should precede the drill.
- Instruct the defenders in the collision area not to be abusive as they *jam* the running back.

Variation:

- Can be used with a dry football.

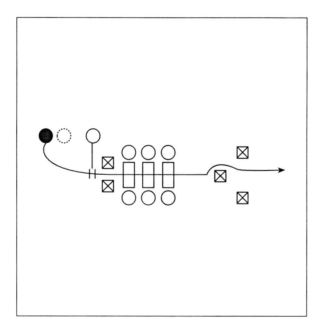

CHAPTER 2

Offensive Line

Drills

DRILL #12: BOARD-DRIVE DRILL

Phillip Fulmer
University of Tennessee
Overall Record: 95-20-0
National Champions: 1998
National Coach of the Year: 1998

Objective: To teach and practice the proper fundamentals and techniques in the execution of the drive block.

Equipment Needed: Five boards (6" x 2" x 8') and five large blocking dummies

Description:

- Place five boards (6" x 2" x 8') perpendicular to a selected line of scrimmage. Approximately five feet separate each board.
- Align an offensive line in three-point stances straddling the midpoint of the boards.
- Position defenders holding dummies in a straddling position across from the offensive line.
- Alternating offensive lines stand behind the performing drill participants.
- On coach's cadence and snap count, the offensive linemen explode out of their stances and execute drive blocks on the defenders, driving them off the end of the boards.
- The defenders react to the movement of the offensive linemen and take a step forward to resist their blocks.
- The drill continues until all offensive lines have had a sufficient number of repetitions.

Coaching Points:

- Always check to see that the linemen are in their proper stances.
- Instruct the linemen to contact the dummy with heads up, shoulders squared to the defender, and feet shoulder-width apart.
- Make sure the linemen use the proper fundamentals and techniques in the execution of the drive block.

Safety Considerations:

- Proper warm-up should precede the drill.
- The drill should progress from walk-through, to half speed, to full speed.
- The coach should monitor closely the intensity of the drill.
- The boards should be beveled and checked for splinters daily.
- Instruct the linemen as to the proper fundamentals and techniques of the drive block.

Variation:

- Can incorporate tight ends.

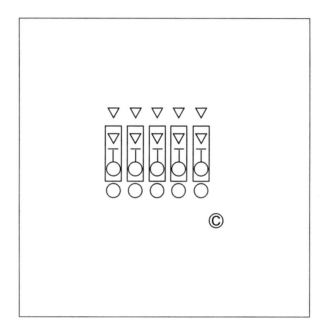

DRILL #13: BODY BALANCE–EQUILIBRIUM–HITTING DRILL

Charles B. "Bud" Wilkinson (Deceased)
University of Oklahoma, St. Louis Cardinals
Overall Record: 154-49-4
National Champions: 1950, 1955, and 1956
National Coach of the Year: 1949
College Football Hall of Fame: 1969
Amos Alonzo Stagg Award: 1984
AFCA President: 1958

Objective: To teach and practice the proper techniques of getting off the ground, regaining balance, and executing a shoulder-drive block.

Equipment Needed: Two-man sled

Description:

- Align two rows of linemen five yards in front of the pads of a two-man sled.

- On the coach's command, the first two drill participants explode from their stances, execute a forward roll, regain their balance, and execute shoulder-drive blocks on the sled.

- After driving the sled for three yards, the linemen disengage the sled and return to the ends of the opposite lines.

- The drill continues until all linemen have executed a sufficient number of forward rolls and left and right shoulder blocks.

Coaching Points:

- Always check to see that the linemen are in their proper stances.

- Insist that the forward roll be performed correctly.

- Instruct linemen to lower their center of gravity, keeping their feet shoulder-width apart as they contact the sled.

- Make sure the linemen use the proper fundamentals and techniques in the execution of all shoulder blocks.

Safety Considerations:

- Proper warm-up should precede the drill.

- The drill area should be clear of all foreign articles.

- Helmets should be worn with chinstraps snapped.

- Instruct the linemen as to the proper fundamentals and techniques of executing the shoulder block and hitting the sled.
- The sled should be checked periodically for possible maintenance and repairs.

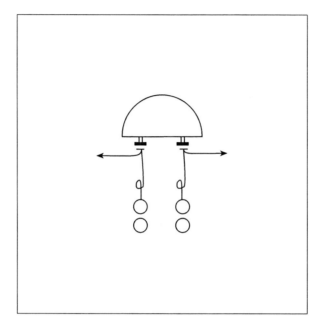

DRILL #14: BREAKDOWN OF THE SHOULDER BLOCK

Harold R. "Tubby" Raymond
University of Delaware
Overall Record: 300-119-3
National Champions: 1971, 1972, and 1979
National Coach of the Year: 1971, 1972, and 1979
AFCA President: 1981

Objective: To teach and practice the proper fundamentals and techniques in the execution of the shoulder block. Special emphasis is placed on identifying the proper *blocking surface.*

Equipment Needed: Large blocking dummies

Description:

- Align all the linemen on their hands and knees in front of a firmly held, large blocking dummy. The drill is conducted in four phases as follows:
    - *Phase one.* On the coach's command, have the linemen demonstrate the *blocking surface* as the front of the shoulder from the neck to the elbow and with the fist in contact with the chest having the shoulders parallel to the ground. The *blocking surface* should be demonstrated for both the left- and right-shoulder blocks.
    - *Phase two.* On the coach's command, all the linemen explode from the waist driving the right shoulder and forearm into the dummy using the *blocking surface* as described in phase one. The technique is repeated with the left shoulder.
    - *Phase three.* The linemen stand in a football position one-step away from the held dummy. On the coach's command, all the linemen step with their left foot and drive their right shoulders and forearms into the dummy using the proper *blocking surface.* The technique is repeated stepping with the right foot and blocking with left shoulder.
    - *Phase four.* The linemen are positioned a short distance from the front of the held dummy. On the coach's command, all the linemen run to and execute a right-shoulder block on the dummy. The technique is repeated using a left-shoulder block.
- The drill continues until all the linemen have had a sufficient number of repetitions in executing the four phases.

Coaching Points:

- Always check to see that the linemen are in the desired stance for the execution of each of the four phases.
- Instruct the linemen to keep their shoulders square to the dummy throughout all phases of the drill.
- Insist that the linemen maintain good hitting positions with the head up and feet shoulder-width apart.
- Check for the proper *blocking surface* on the dummies after each block.

Safety Considerations:

- Proper warm-up should precede the drill.
- The drill area should be clear of all foreign articles.
- Helmets should be worn with chinstraps snapped.
- Instruct the dummy holders to maintain a firm grip on the dummies.

Variation:

- Can be used for all positions.

DRILL #15: CHUTE DRILL

Alonzo S. "Jake" Gaither (Deceased)
Florida A&M University
Overall Record: 203-36-4
National College Black Champions: 1950, 1952, 1954, 1957, 1959, and 1961
National Coach of the Year: 1961 and 1969
College Football Hall of Fame: 1975
Amos Alonzo Stagg Award: 1974

Objective: To teach and practice the proper fundamentals and techniques of driving out of the stance. Special emphasis is placed on cadence recognition, stance, and maintaining the proper body position.

Equipment Needed: Blocking chute (seven stalls - 36" high x 48" wide), seven boards (14" x 2" x 6'), and footballs

Description:

- Place a board in each of the starting stalls of the blocking chute.
- Align the offensive linemen in waves behind the stalls of the blocking chute.
- The coach stands at either end of the chute.
- On the coach's command, the first wave of linemen take their stances under the chute with the center over the football in the middle stall. A quarterback is positioned over the center.
- On the quarterback's cadence and ball snap, all the linemen drive out of their stances.
- The drill continues until all the linemen have had a sufficient number of repetitions.

Coaching Points:

- Make sure all the linemen are aligned correctly and are in their proper stances.
- Insist that the linemen maintain good body alignment throughout the drill.
- Insist that the drill be conducted at full speed.

Safety Considerations:

- Proper warm-up should precede the drill.
- The drill area should be clear of all foreign articles.

- It is imperative that helmets be worn with chinstraps snapped.
- The boards should be beveled and checked for splinters daily.

Variations:

- Can be used with the linemen driving out of their stances at varying distances behind the blocking chute.
- Can be used with the linemen driving out of their stances and blocking dummies.
- Can be used as a tight-end drill.

DRILL #16: DRIVE-TURN

Joe V. Paterno
Pennsylvania State University
Overall Record: 327-96-3
National Champions: 1982 and 1986
National Coach of the Year: 1968, 1978, 1981, 1982, 1986, 1990, 1994 and 1998
Amos Alonzo Stagg Award: 2002

Objective: To teach and practice the proper fundamentals and techniques of maintaining contact with a defender after the initial block.

Equipment Needed: Two-man sled

Description:

- Position a row of linemen in front of the left pad of a two-man blocking sled.
- The coach stands adjacent to the opposite pad and fixes his hands on the strut.
- On the coach's cadence and snap count, the first lineman drives out of his stance and executes a right-shoulder block to the pad of the sled.
- Just after the lineman begins to drive the sled, the coach turns the sled by pushing and pulling on the strut.
- The drill continues until all the linemen have had a sufficient number of repetitions with both left- and right-shoulder blocks.

Coaching Points:

- Always check to see that linemen are in their proper stances.
- Instruct the linemen to contact the sled with their shoulders square to the pad, heads up, and feet apart.
- It is important that all linemen accelerate their feet and turn their heads into the strut in maintaining control over the sled.
- Make sure the linemen use the proper fundamentals and techniques in the execution of all shoulder blocks.

Safety Considerations:

- Proper warm-up should precede the drill.
- The drill area should be clear of all foreign articles.
- Helmets should be worn with chinstraps snapped.

- The coach should not manipulate the sled until the lineman has made contact and has the sled under control.
- The coach should never jerk or move the sled too hard or too rapidly.
- The sled should be checked periodically for possible maintenance and repairs.

Variation:

- Can be used without the coach holding the strut.

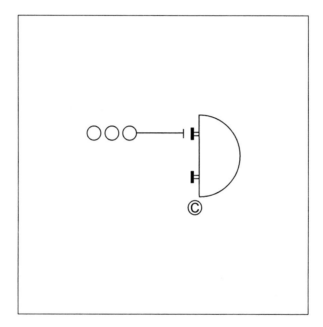

DRILL #17: ONE-MAN SLED DRIVE TECHNIQUE

Dal Shealy
Mars Hill College, Carson-Newman College, University of Richmond
Overall Record: 87-54-0
Fellowship of Christian Athletes: President and CEO

Objective: To teach and practice the proper fundamentals and techniques in the execution of the drive block.

Equipment Needed: One-man blocking sled

Description:

- Position all the offensive linemen in a straight line in front of a one-man blocking sled. The drill is conducted in three phases as follows:
  - *Six-point stance* (on hands and knees with toes curled up under feet). On the coach's cadence and snap count, the first lineman explodes into the pad of the sled with a right-shoulder drive block. Special emphasis should be placed on rolling the hips. The procedure is repeated with all the linemen, in turn, executing both left- and right-shoulder drive blocks.
  - *Four-point stance.* On the coach's cadence and snap count, the first lineman explodes from his stance and executes a right-shoulder block on the pad of the sled. Special emphasis is placed on rolling the hips and forming a *power angle* with the forearm. The sled is driven five to eight yards. Procedure is repeated with all linemen, in turn, executing both left- and right-shoulder drive blocks.
  - *Three-point stance.* Same as the preceding procedure except all the shoulder-drive blocks are executed from a three-point stance.
- The drill continues until all the linemen have had a sufficient number of repetitions in executing the three phases of the drill.

Coaching Points:

- Always check to see that all the linemen are in their proper stances.
- In contacting the sled, emphasize the importance of rolling the hips and forming the *power angle*.
- Instruct the linemen to keep their shoulders squared to the sled throughout all phases of the drill.
- Insist that the linemen maintain a good hitting position with their heads up and feet shoulder-width apart.

- When driving the sled, all the linemen should take short driving steps.
- Make sure the linemen practice the proper fundamentals and techniques in the execution of all shoulder blocks.

Safety Considerations:

- Proper warm-up should precede the drill.
- The drill area should be clear of all foreign articles.
- Helmets should be worn with chinstraps snapped.
- The sled should be checked periodically for possible maintenance and repairs.

Variations:

- Can be used for over-and-up, scoop, reach, and wheel blocks.
- Can align blockers three-yards off sled to simulate blocking on a linebacker.

DRILL #18: PULL FOR SWEEP

William G. "Bill" Dooley
University of North Carolina, Virginia Polytechnic Institute, Wake Forest University
Overall Record: 162-126-5

Objective: To teach and practice the proper fundamentals and techniques of pulling. Incorporated are skills related to agility, body control, reaction, and quickness.

Equipment Needed: Five cones, four hand shields, and footballs

Description:

- Place five cones—one each at the noseguard, guard, and tackle positions—on a selected line of scrimmage. Position two linebackers and two defensive ends, holding hand shields, in their regular alignments (see diagram).
- Align two offensive guards in their normal positions.
- A tailback, holding a football, is positioned six-yards deep in the backfield.
- Other drill participants stand adjacent to drill area.
- On the coach's cadence and snap count, the offensive personnel execute a designated sweep play utilizing various pulling schemes.
- The defenders react and move according to their basic sweep reads.
- The drill continues until all drill participants have run a sufficient number of repetitions.
- The drill should be run from both left and right formations and from various field positions.

Coaching Points:

- Always check to see that all the drill participants are aligned correctly and are in their proper stances.
- In the execution of the *step-out*, make sure that all linemen pull their onside arm back hard, keeping the elbow as close to the hip as possible.
- Instruct pulling linemen to look for their defenders on their first step.
- Instruct linemen as to the principles of the pulling curve.
- Make sure the linemen use the proper fundamentals and techniques of pulling and blocking.
- Insist that the tailbacks read the defensive end correctly so the linebackers will be in the correct positions for the blocks by the pulling linemen.

Safety Considerations:

- Proper warm-up should precede the drill.
- The drill area should be clear of all foreign articles.
- The drill should progress from half speed to full speed.
- The coach should monitor closely the intensity of the drill.
- Instruct the linemen as to the proper fundamentals and techniques of pulling and blocking.
- Review the different pulling schemes with the defenders and remind them to remain alert.

Variations:

- Can be used as a form or live pulling-and-blocking drill.
- Can incorporate other offensive personnel.
- Can be used for lead and kick-out plays.
- Can be used as a defensive end and linebacker drill.

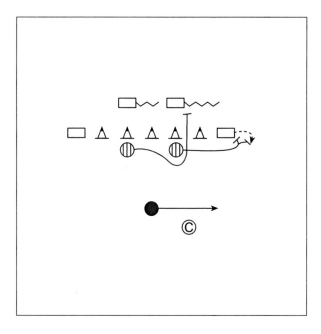

DRILL #19: LINE PUNCH

Dennis "Fran" Franchione
Texas Christian University, University of New Mexico,
Southwest Texas State University, Pittsburg State University,
Southwestern College, University of Alabama
Overall Record: 145-70-2
National Coach of the Year: Pittsburg State 1987 and 1987

Objective: To teach and practice the proper fundamentals in executing the punch technique in pass blocking.

Equipment Needed: Five-man or seven-man blocking sled

Description:

- Align a row of offensive linemen adjacent and parallel to a five- or seven-man blocking sled. All the linemen are facing the sled (see diagram).

- On the coach's command, the first lineman slides in front of the first sled pad and executes the *punch* technique. He then slides laterally to the second sled pad and executes another *punch* technique. He continues until he has executed the *punch* technique on each sled pad.

- When the first lineman has completed his slide through and *punching*, the second lineman takes his turn, etc.

- The drill continues until all the linemen have had a sufficient number of repetitions moving from both the left and the right on the sled.

Coaching Points:

- Instruct the linemen as to the proper fundamentals and techniques of executing the *punch* technique.

- Make sure the linemen focus on the target area of the pad as they execute the *punch*.

- Emphasize that the speed of the slide between the pads is not as important as the execution of the *punch*.

- Insist that the linemen maintain a good *punching* position with their head up, eyes focused on the target area, and feet shoulder-width apart as they slide from one pad to another.

Safety Considerations:

- Proper warm-up should precede the drill.
- The sled should be checked periodically for possible maintenance and repairs.
- The drill should progress from formwork to full speed.

Variation:

- Can be used with a row of defenders aligned facing the offensive linemen. Drill participants should be two-feet apart and the offensive linemen should be instructed to step forward as they executes the *punch* technique on the forward-stepping defender.

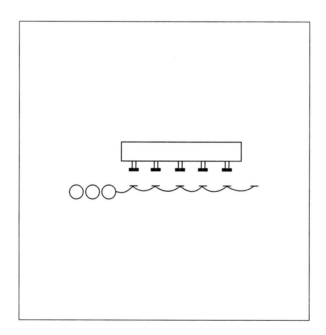

CHAPTER 3

Quarterback Ballhandling and

Passing Drills

DRILL #20: CIRCLE DRILL

The Honorable Dr. Thomas "Tom" Osborne
University of Nebraska
Overall Record: 255-49-3
National Champions: 1994, 1995, and 1997
National Coach of the Year: 1978, 1983, 1994, and 1995
Fellowship of Christian Athletes Grant Teaff Coach of the Year: 1997
College Football Hall of Fame: 1998
Amos Alonzo Stagg Award: 2000

Objective: To teach and practice the proper mechanics of passing a football while running in a circle. Special emphasis is placed on maintaining the correct body alignment.

Equipment Needed: Footballs

Description:

- Align paired quarterbacks with a football 15-yards apart as shown in the diagram.
- On the first command, the paired quarterbacks circle in a counterclockwise direction passing the football back and forth to each other.
- On the second command, the paired quarterbacks change direction and execute their passes while running in a clockwise direction.
- The drill continues until all quarterbacks have thrown a sufficient number of passes.

Coaching Points:

- Instruct all the quarterbacks to keep the football above the shoulders as they circle.
- Insist that all the quarterbacks draw their hips and square their shoulders as each pass is thrown.
- Make sure all the quarterbacks practice the proper mechanics in throwing all passes.

Safety Considerations:

- Proper warm-up should precede the drill.
- The drill area should be clear of all foreign articles.
- Maintain a safe distance between each pair of paired drill participants.

Variation:

- Can vary the distance between the paired quarterbacks.

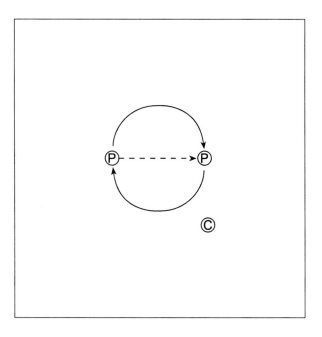

DRILL #21: DROP-BACK DRILL

Jim J. Sweeney
Montana State University, Washington State University,
California State University at Fresno
Overall Record: 196-147-4

Objective: To teach and practice the proper mechanics in the execution of the three-step, five-step, and seven-step pass drops.

Equipment Needed: Footballs

Description:

- Align a quarterback with a football in a post-snap position on a selected line of scrimmage.
- Other quarterbacks stand adjacent to the drill area.
- The coach stands directly in front of quarterback in a front-facing position.
- On the cadence and snap count, the quarterback executes a three-step pass drop and sets to pass. The quarterback now sprints back to his post-snap alignment and procedure is repeated two more times. This completes the three-step pass-drop set phase of the drill.
- The drill continues, repeating procedure four for the five-step and seven-step pass drops.
- After the third set of seven-step pass drops is completed, the quarterback works his feet in place and the coach signals him to sprint left or right.
- The drill continues until all the quarterbacks have had a sufficient number of repetitions.

Coaching Points:

- Always check to see that the quarterbacks are in their proper stances.
- Make sure all the quarterbacks execute each pass drop correctly.
- Always check for the proper ball position as the quarterback sets to pass.

Safety Consideration:

- Proper warm-up should precede the drill.

Variations:

- Can be used with a center snap.
- Can incorporate all the quarterbacks in the drill at the same time.
- Can have the quarterback pass the football to a receiver after each pass drop.

DRILL #22: OVER-THE-TOP PASSING

Robert C. "Bobby" Bowden
Samford University, West Virginia University, Florida State University
Overall Record: 323-91-4
National Champions: Florida State 1993 and 1999
National Coach of the Year: Florida State 1979, 1980, 1991 1996, and 1999
Fellowship of Christian Athletes Grant Teaff Coach of the Year: 2000

Objective: To teach and practice the proper mechanics of passing the football up and over a defensive back in the execution of the take-off route.

Equipment Needed: Footballs

Description:

- Align a center and a quarterback over the football in the middle of the field on the 50-yard line.
- A wide receiver is positioned on the line of scrimmage in the middle of the right outside third of the field. His back foot is placed on the 50-yard line.
- A defensive back is placed with his back to the quarterback and one yard to the inside of the receiver. His front foot is placed on the 50-yard line.
- Other drill participants stand adjacent to their drill area.
- On the cadence and ball snap, the quarterback takes a three-step pass drop as the receiver runs the take-off route with the defensive back in chase.
- The quarterback passes the football 35 yards downfield and over-the-top of the defender and the receiver catches the ball over his outside shoulder.
- The drill continues until all the quarterbacks have thrown a sufficient number of over-the-top passes.
- The drill should be run both left and right.

Coaching Points:

- Always check to see that the quarterbacks are aligned correctly.
- Make sure the center-quarterback exchange is executed properly.
- Make sure all the quarterbacks get plenty of *loft* on each pass.
- Instruct the receivers to sprint full speed staying to the outside of the defenders.
- Insist that all the defenders stay as close to the receivers as possible, thus forcing a perfect pass.
- Make sure all the quarterbacks practice proper mechanics in throwing all passes.

Safety Considerations:

- Proper warm-up should precede the drill.
- The drill area should be clear of all foreign articles. This includes the sideline areas.
- This drill is not recommended as a contact drill.
- Instruct returning drill participants to stay clear of the drill area.

Variations:

- Can be conducted from either hash mark as well as midfield.
- Can be used as a wide-receiver drill.
- Can be used as a defensive-back drill.
- Can be used as a center-quarterback ball-exchange drill.

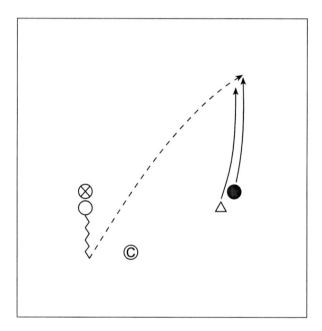

DRILL #23: SHORT-STEP CARIOCA

Steve Spurrier
Tampa Bay Bandits, Duke University, University of Florida, Washington Redskins
Overall Record: 177-59-2
National Champions: Florida 1996
National Coach of the Year: Florida 1996

Objective: To teach and practice foot speed, proper head position, viewing the field, and holding the football for a straight drop-back pass.

Equipment Needed: Footballs

Description:

- Align all the quarterbacks five-yards apart on a selected line of scrimmage. Each drill participant holds a football at the post-snap position.

- On the designated quarterback's cadence and snap count, all the quarterbacks pull the balls to and across their chests as each retreats 15 yards using short *carioca* steps (*carioca* stepping is executed at full speed).

- The quarterbacks return to the original line of scrimmage and the procedure is repeated.

- The drill continues until all the quarterbacks have executed a sufficient number of repetitions.

Coaching Points:

- Always check to see that the quarterbacks are in their proper stances.

- Insist that all the quarterbacks pull the football to and across their chests from the post-snap position.

- Make sure the drill is performed at full speed.

- The coach should monitor and record the number of *carioca* steps each quarterback takes in his fifteen-yard pass drop.

- Instruct all the quarterbacks to cock their heads as far to the left as possible, focusing on an object high and far away as they execute their pass drops (right-handed quarterback).

Safety Considerations:

- Proper warm-up should precede the drill.

- The drill area should be clear of all foreign articles.

- Instruct all personnel as to the correct techniques in performing the *carioca* stepping.
- Maintain a minimum distance of five yards between performing drill participants.

Variations:

- Can be used with various quarterback drops.
- Can incorporate a center and use as a center-quarterback ball-exchange drill.

DRILL #24: STEP-AND-THROW DRILL

R. LaVell Edwards
Brigham Young University
Overall Record: 257-101-3
National Champions: 1984
National Coach of the Year: 1984
AFCA President: 1987

Objective: To teach and practice taking the proper step angle in passing the football to a particular receiver. Incorporated are skills of setting-up, reading, quickness, and agility.

Equipment Needed: Footballs

Description:

- Align a quarterback and a center over the football at the midpoint of a selected line of scrimmage.
- Place four receivers at ending positions of a designated pass pattern (see diagram).
- Other quarterbacks stand adjacent to the drill area or serve as receivers.
- On the cadence and ball snap, the quarterback executes his pass drop according to the play called and follows his proper read progression against a designated (simulated) coverage.
- The coach who is positioned behind the quarterback signals to one of the four receivers to raise his hand.
- As the designated receiver raises his hand, the quarterback passes him the football.
- The drill continues until all the quarterbacks have had a sufficient number of repetitions.
- The drill should be run from both the left and right hash marks as well as from midfield.

Coaching Points:

- Always check to see that the quarterbacks are in their proper stances.
- Make sure the center-quarterback exchange is executed correctly.
- Instruct the quarterbacks to follow their read progression with each pass thrown.
- Insist that all the quarterbacks continue to shuffle their feet as they complete their read progression.

- Make sure all the quarterbacks take the proper stepping angle when throwing to a particular receiver.
- Make sure all the quarterbacks practice the proper mechanics in throwing all passes.

Safety Considerations:

- Proper warm-up should precede the drill.
- The drill area should be clear of all foreign articles.

Variations:

- Can be used with various quarterback-pass drops and receiver alignments.
- Can incorporate a hot pass when the quarterback has to alter his pass drop.

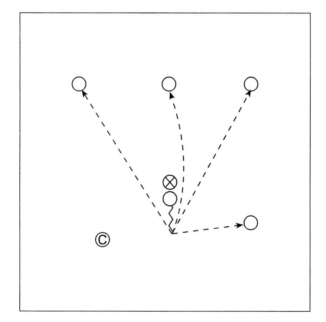

DRILL #25: WAVE DRILL

Bob Ford
St. Lawrence University, University at Albany
Overall Record: 180-130-2
AFCA President: 2000

Objective: To teach and practice the skills of moving forward and laterally in avoiding a pass rush while keeping the football at the *ready-to-pass* position.

Equipment Needed: Footballs

Description:

- Align two rows of quarterbacks 15-yards apart and facing one another on two selected lines of scrimmage. Five yards should separate the quarterbacks on the same line of scrimmage (see diagram).
- The coach is positioned in the middle of the drill area.
- On a designated quarterback's cadence and snap count, all the quarterbacks on his line of scrimmage execute a five-step pass drop.
- When this row of quarterbacks takes their fifth drop step, the coach waves for them to move either to their left or to their right.
- After the row of quarterbacks has moved to either the left or the right, the coach now signals the quarterbacks to pass the football to the front-facing quarterbacks in the opposite row by bringing his hand forward and to the ground.
- The drill continues until the alternating rows of quarterbacks have had a sufficient number of repetitions moving both to the left and the right.

Coaching Points:

- Always check to see that the quarterbacks are in their proper stance.
- Make sure that the quarterbacks' five-step drops are executed correctly.
- Insist that the quarterbacks always practice the proper mechanics in throwing all passes.
- Insist that the quarterbacks always keep their feet, shoulders, and throwing arm in the *ready-to-pass* position throughout the drill.
- Instruct the quarterbacks to always have both hands on the football and to be ready to move either to the left or the right, and to throw the football on the coach's signal.

Safety Considerations:

- Proper warm-up should precede the drill.
- The drill area should be clear of all foreign articles.
- The coach should make sure he is never in the *line of fire* of the quarterbacks' passes.

Variations:

- Can be used with a variety of pass drops, sprint outs, and rollouts.
- The coach can wave the quarterback from side to side before signaling for the passes to be thrown.
- The coach can signal the quarterback to pass the football after the quarterbacks completes their initial five-step drop.
- The coach can signal the quarterbacks to move forward before passing the football.

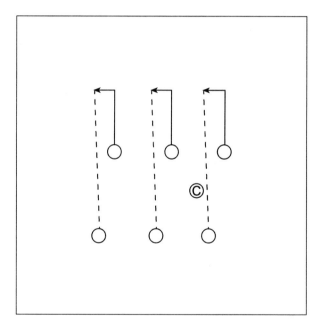

CHAPTER 4

Tight End

Drills

DRILL #26: HASH

Joseph Dennis "Joe" Taylor
Howard University, Virginia Union University, Hampton University
Overall Record: 146-54-4
National Black College Champions: Hampton 1994 and 1997
National Black College Coach of the Year: 1994 and 1997
AFCA President: 2001

Objective: To teach and practice the proper techniques in getting open in the underneath hash area.

Equipment Needed: Three large blocking dummies and footballs

Description:

- Align rows of tight ends perpendicular to and five-yards inside and outside the right hash mark on a selected line of scrimmage.

- Position-held dummies 12-yards downfield on the hash mark and five yards to the left and right of the hash marks.

- A quarterback holding a football is positioned on the line of scrimmage between the two lines of receivers.

- On the quarterback's cadence and snap count, the designated tight end releases from the line and works the space between the two dummies on his side of the hash marks. If the quarterback does not pass him the football between the first two dummies, the tight end works for a position between the other pair of dummies and away from pressure.

- The quarterback is instructed to execute a designated pass drop and pass the football to the tight end between either pair of held dummies or away from pressure.

- After catching the pass, the tight end turns and sprints upfield. He then returns to the opposite receiving line.

- The drill continues until all the tight ends have had a sufficient number of repetitions.

- The drill should be conducted from both the left and right hash marks and from various field positions.

Coaching Points:

- Always check to see that the tight ends are aligned correctly and are in their proper stances.

- Instruct the tight ends to execute their release techniques (rip or swim) correctly.

- Insist that all the tight ends maintain a good *football position* as they work to get open between the dummies. (Instruct tight ends to move laterally without drifting in depth.)

- Insist that the drill be conducted at full speed.

Safety Considerations:

- Proper warm-up should precede the drill.

- The drill area should be clear of all foreign articles.

- Helmets should be worn with chinstraps snapped.

Variations:

- Can be used with a defender holding a hand shield over the tight end to prevent his release off the line.

- Can be used as a wide-receiver drill.

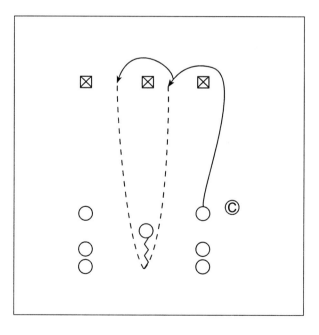

DRILL #27: TIGHT END BLOCKING

James M. "Jim" Christopherson
Concordia College (Moorhead)
Overall Record: 218-101-7
National Champions: 1978 and 1981
National Coach of the Year: 1981

Objective: To teach and practice the proper fundamentals and techniques in blocking the gap, reach, and arch blocks.

Equipment Needed: None

Description:

- Align a tight end in his stance on a selected line of scrimmage.
- Position a defensive end or a linebacker in his normal alignment over the tight end.
- Other drill participants will stand adjacent to the drill area.
- On the quarterback's (coach's) cadence and snap count, the tight end executes the designated blocking technique that was called in the huddle (gap, reach, or arch). (See the following diagrams.)
- The drill continues until all the tight ends have had a sufficient number of repetitions executing the gap, reach, and arch blocks.
- The drill should be conducted from both left and right formations.

Coaching Points:

- Always check to see that the tight ends are aligned correctly and are in their proper stance.
- Instruct the tight ends on the proper techniques in executing the gap, reach, and arch blocks. This is especially true in regard to footwork.
- In the execution of the gap and reach blocks, emphasis should be placed on making contact at the correct *blocking point* on the defender.
- In executing the reach block, the tight ends should be instructed to *jolt* the defensive end before maneuvering their body into an outside blocking position.
- The emphasis of drill should be on repetition and not contact.

Safety Considerations:

- Proper warm-up should precede the drill.
- The drill should progress from formwork to live work.
- Helmets should be worn and chinstraps snapped.
- The drill area should be clear of all foreign articles.

Variation:

- Can be used as a defensive-end, linebacker, and defensive-back drill.

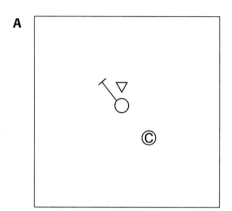

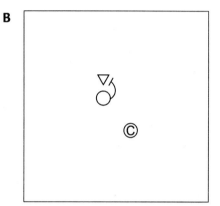

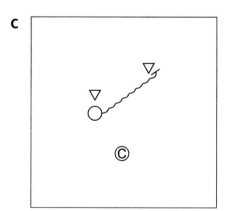

DRILL #28: SPEED RELEASE

Roger N. Harring
University of Wisconsin-La Crosse
Overall Record: 261-74-8
National Champions: 1985, 1992, and 1995
National Coach of the Year: 1992 and 1995

Objective: To teach the proper use of the hands in executing the *speed* release. Incorporated are skills related to quickness and concentration.

Equipment Needed: Large plastic wiffleball bat

Description:

- Align a row of tight ends on a selected line of scrimmage. Approximately one yard separates the tight ends (see diagram).

- The coach, holding a wiffleball bat, positions himself in front of the row of tight ends.

- On the coach's command, all the tight ends assume the quarter-eagle football position while *buzzing* their feet.

- The coach now walks directly toward the row of tight ends pointing the wiffleball bat at the outside numbers of each drill participant. (The coach is simulating a defensive end's attempt to grab and hold up the tight end's release.)

- As the coach walks toward each tight end in sequence, the tight ends execute a quick slap with the outside hand, knocking the wiffleball bat out of the way. Simultaneously, the tight ends turn their hips and shoulders as each executes a *carioca* step to clear their hips past the coach (defender).

- After the coach passes the last tight end in the row, the drill is repeated with the tight ends now facing the opposite direction.

- The drill continues until all the tight ends have had a sufficient number of repetitions using both the left and right hand slaps.

Coaching Points:

- Always check to see that the tight ends are in the quarter-eagle position and are *buzzing* their feet.

- Instruct all the tight ends to use the proper hand-slap technique.

- Emphasize the importance of the tight ends working to clear their hips while simultaneously delivering the hand slap.

Safety Considerations:

- Proper warm-up should precede the drill.
- Helmets should be worn with chinstraps snapped.
- The wiffleball bat should be checked periodically for cracks and rough spots.

Variations:

- Can be used with the offensive ends coming out of a three-point stance.
- Can be used as a wide-receiver drill in teaching the release against a *jam* corner.
- Can incorporate a quarterback and execute a designated pass route after the release.

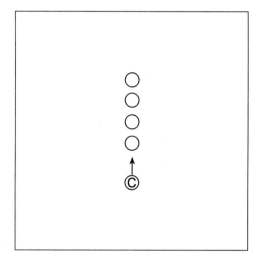

DRILL #29: SIX CONES AND A FOOTBALL

Richard "Dick" Farley
Williams College
Overall Record: 101-16-3

Objective: To teach and practice the proper fundamentals and techniques of accelerating in and out of various passing-route break points, catching the football, and eluding a downfield defender.

Equipment Needed: Six cones and a football

Description:

- Place four cones seven-yards apart in the shape of a square. A fifth cone is placed in the middle of the square and a sixth cone is placed seven-yards behind the fifth cone.

- Align a row of tight ends to the right of and behind the cone on the right side of the square. Place a defender in front of the cone positioned behind the square (see diagram).

- The quarterback (coach) is positioned to the left of the line of tight ends and in the normal quarterback-tight end relationship.

- On the quarterback's (coach's) cadence and snap count, the first tight end drives from his stance and sprints past the upfield cone. As he passes the upfield cone, he executes the designated pass route (curl, hitch, or dig) and catches the football thrown by the coach. (See Diagram A for the curl and hitch pattern; see Diagram B for the dig pattern.)

- After catching the football, the tight end turns around and sprints toward the defender positioned in front of the back cone and executes a full-speed double move, beating the defender on the outside.

- The drill continues until all the tight ends have had a sufficient number of repetitions.

- The drill should be conducted with the tight ends running the curl, hitch, and dig patterns from both the left and right side of the squares.

Coaching Points:

- Always check to see that the tight ends are aligned correctly and are in their proper stance.

- Instruct all the tight ends to drop their hips, plant their outside foot, and drive the outside knee and elbow toward the midpoint when executing the designated pass route.
- Instruct the tight ends to drive to the middle cone when executing the hitch and curl pattern.
- Insist that the tight ends accelerate in and out of all break points.
- Instruct the tight ends to always watch the football into their hands and to *tuck* it away before sprinting downfield.

Safety Considerations:

- Proper warm-up should precede the drill.
- Helmets should be worn and chinstraps snapped.
- The drill should progress from formwork to full speed.

Variations:

- Can be used as a wide-receiver drill.
- Can be used with any pass-route break point that is a part of the offense's passing scheme.

A
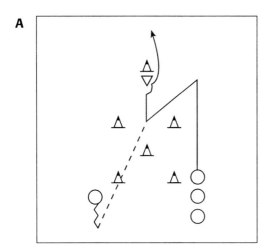

B
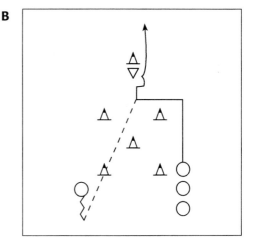

DRILL #30: OUTSIDE RELEASE

Frank L. Girardi
Lycoming College
Overall Record: 226-69-5

Objective: To teach and practice the proper fundamentals and techniques in executing the outside release.

Equipment Needed: Hand shield

Description:

- Align a tight end in his stance on a selected line of scrimmage.
- Position a defender, holding a hand shield, in his normal alignment over the tight end.
- Other drill participants stand adjacent to the drill area.
- On the quarterback's (coach's) cadence and snap count, the tight end executes his outside release technique as the defender *jams* him with the hand shield in an effort to prevent his release.
- The drill continues until all the tight ends have had a sufficient number of repetitions using various outside release techniques from both left and right formations.

Coaching Points:

- Always check to see that the tight ends are in their proper stances.
- Instruct the tight ends to first take a lateral step with the outside foot, and then lead through with the inside arm and leg while keeping the shoulders squared.
- The position of the defender should vary from a head-up position to an outside alignment over the tight end.
- After their release from the line of scrimmage, instruct the tight ends to get into their designated pass route as quickly as possible.

Safety Considerations:

- Proper warm-up should precede the drill.
- Helmets should be worn and chinstraps snapped.
- The drill should progress from formwork to live work.

- The coach should monitor closely the intensity of the drill.
- Instruct the defenders not to be overly aggressive in preventing the tight end's release and never to *jam* the tight end in the head area.

Variations:

- Can be used as a slot-back outside-release drill.
- Can be used as a defensive-end or outside-linebacker drill.

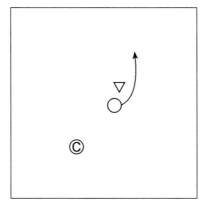

DRILL #31: TWO-LEVEL RELEASE

Jim Tressel
Youngstown State University, The Ohio State University
Overall Record: 142-63-2
National Champions: Youngstown State 1991, 1993, 1994, and 1997
National Coach of the Year: Youngstown State 1991, 1993, 1994, and 1997

Objective: To teach and practice the proper fundamentals and techniques in executing line releases and linebacker-level releases. Incorporated are skills related to pass catching and concentration.

Equipment Needed: Four arm shields, a cone, and footballs

Description:

- Position a tight end in his stance on a selected line of scrimmage. A cone is placed at the center position.

- Defenders holding arm shields are positioned one over the outside shoulder of the tight end, another at the onside linebacker position, and two others at the end of the designated pass route (hook pattern - see diagram).

- Other tight ends stand adjacent to the drill area.

- A coach holding a football is aligned behind the center (cone) at the appropriate quarterback pass drop alignment.

- On the coach's cadence and snap count, the tight end releases off the line of scrimmage executing either the *rip*, *swim*, or *counter-rip/swim* technique as the defensive end *jams* the tight end in an effort to prevent the release.

- After gaining a release from the line of scrimmage, the tight end continues upfield and executes the *rip-and-drive*, the *stick-and-club*, or *speed* technique on the linebacker. The linebacker who is reading the tight end's release move to his outside *jams* the tight end in an effort to prevent his release at the second level.

- After clearing the linebacker the tight end continues upfield running the designated *hook* pattern. As the tight end comes out of his pass route break point, he drives between the two downfield defenders, and the coach passes him the pass as the two defenders attempt to disrupt the tight end by *jamming* him as he makes the catch.

- After the catch is made, the tight end *tucks* the football away and sprints upfield.

- The drill continues until all the tight ends have had a sufficient number of repetitions from both the left and right alignments.

Coaching Points:

- Always check to see that the tight ends are aligned correctly and are in their proper stances.

- In executing the *rip* technique, instruct the tight ends to take a lateral step to the side of the release and then drive their release-side shoulder under the defensive end and *power up* through the level.

- In executing the *swim* technique, instruct the tight ends to pin the defensive end's release-side elbow toward his hip and swim with the opposite arm over the top.

- In executing the *counter/rip-swim technique*, instruct the tight ends to head-and-shoulder fake the defensive end in the opposite direction before executing the release.

- In executing the *rip-and-drive technique*, instruct the tight ends to execute a rip while driving through the linebacker.

- In executing the *stick-and-club technique*, instruct the tight ends to head fake opposite and *club* the linebacker's arm to the hip before *ripping* upfield.

- In executing the *speed* technique, instruct the tight ends to beat the linebacker to the release point.

- Instruct the tight ends to always maintain a vertical push upfield and not to get re-routed by the defensive end or linebacker.

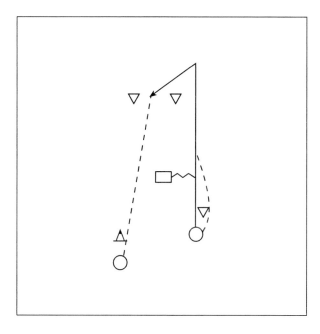

Safety Considerations:

- Proper warm-up should precede drill.
- The drill area should be clear of all foreign articles.
- The coach should monitor closely the intensity of the drill.
- Instruct all the defenders not to be overly aggressive and not to *jam* the tight ends in the head area.
- Instruct the tight ends as to the proper fundamentals and techniques in executing the different releases.
- The drill should progress from walk through to full speed.

Variation:

- Can be used as a defensive-end and strong-side linebacker drill.

CHAPTER 5

Wide Receiver

Drills

DRILL #32: CONE DRILL

Paul "Bear" Bryant (Deceased)
[Drill submitted by Ray Perkins]
University of Maryland, University of Kentucky, Texas A&M University,
University of Alabama
Overall Record: 323-85-17
National Champions: Alabama 1961, 1964, 1965, 1973, 1978, and 1979
National Coach of the Year: Alabama 1961, 1971, and 1973
College Football Hall of Fame: 1986
Amos Alonzo Stagg Award: 1983
AFCA President: 1972

Objective: To teach and practice the proper fundamentals and techniques of coming off a pass cut at full speed and catching the football.

Equipment Needed: Four cones and footballs

Description:

- Align four cones 10-yards apart in a square as shown in the diagram.
- Position all receivers in a straight line behind one of the cones.
- The coach stands in the middle of the drill area holding a football.
- On the coach's command (raising the football), the first receiver drives from his stance and sprints to and executes a 90-degree turn around the first cone. As he makes the turn, he looks for a pass thrown by the coach.
- This procedure continues around the remaining two cones with the coach throwing the receiver the pass after any one of his 90-degree cuts.
- The drill continues until all the receivers have had a sufficient number of repetitions.
- The drill should be conducted with the receivers running both clockwise and counterclockwise around the square.

Coaching Points:

- Make sure that the receivers plant and cut off their outside foot in executing each 90-degree turn.
- Insist that all the receivers run at full speed and only come under control approximately two and one-half yards from each cone.

- Emphasize the importance of exploding off the cut and getting the head around as quickly as possible.
- Insist that the receivers catch all the passes with their hands.

Safety Considerations:

- Proper warm-up should precede the drill.
- Helmets should be worn with chinstraps snapped.

Variations:

- Can be used to practice the 45-degree comeback pattern.
- Can be used as a tight end and running back drill.

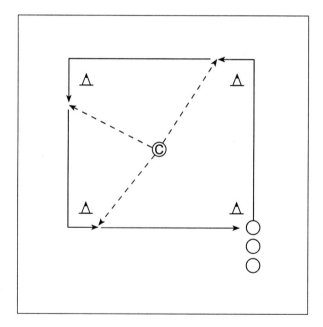

DRILL #33: NET-FLASH DRILL

Ken W. Hatfield
United States Air Force Academy, University of Arkansas,
Clemson University, Rice University
Overall Record: 155-108-4
National Coach of the Year: Air Force 1983
Fellowship of Christian Athletes Grant Teaff Coach of the Year: 2001

Objective: To teach and practice the proper fundamentals and techniques of catching the football with special emphasis on hand-eye coordination, concentration, and protecting the football.

Equipment Needed: Goal post net, two hand shields, and footballs

Description:

- Position a receiver in the middle of the end zone facing a netted goalpost.
- Shield holders are positioned on both sides of the receiver.
- The quarterback (coach) stands ten yards from the receiver.
- Alternating drill participants stand adjacent to the drill area.
- On the quarterback's (coach's) command, the receiver executes a 180-degree turn and catches the pass thrown by the quarterback.
- The receiver now tucks the football under the arm opposite the way he turned (if receiver turns to his right, the football is tucked under the left arm) as the shield holder on the side of the football *jams* him with his shield.
- The drill continues until all the receivers have had a sufficient number of catches turning to both their left and right.

Coaching Points:

- Instruct all the receivers to turn their heads first and then their bodies.
- Make sure that the receivers watch the football into their hands.
- Insist that the receivers tuck and cover the football completely after each reception is made.

Safety Considerations:

- Proper warm-up should precede the drill.
- Helmets should be worn with chinstraps snapped.
- Full equipment should be worn.
- Instruct the shield holder not to *jam* the receiver in the head area.

Variations:

- Can be used as a tight end and running back drill.
- Can be used as a defensive back, linebacker, and defensive end drill.
- Passes can be thrown at different heights and with varying velocities.

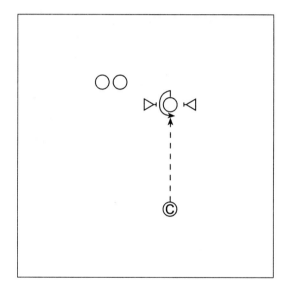

DRILL #34: RELEASE DRILL

J. Hayden Fry
Southern Methodist University, North Texas State University, University of Iowa
Overall Record: 232-178-10
National Coach of the Year: Iowa 1981
AFCA President: 1993

Objective: To teach and practice the proper fundamentals and techniques in releasing from the line of scrimmage.

Equipment Needed: Hand shield and footballs

Description:

- Align receivers five-yards apart on a selected line of scrimmage.
- A defender with a hand shield is positioned at various depths either inside, outside, or head-up each receiver. He is instructed to prevent the release of the receiver.
- On the coach's cadence and snap count, the receiver executes one of four release techniques (A - inside, B - outside, C- roll-out, and D - roll-in) as designated by the coach (see diagram).
- After the designated release technique is executed, the receiver carries out his regular blocking or pass play assignment.
- The drill continues until all the receivers have executed a sufficient number of line releases.
- The drill should be conducted from both left and right formations.

Coaching Points:

- Always check to see that the receivers are aligned correctly and are in their proper stances.
- Instruct the receivers to turn inside and to watch for an imaginary ball snap.
- Insist that the receivers drive off the line of scrimmage as dictated by the depth and alignment of the defenders.
- Instruct all the receivers as to the desired techniques and fundamentals of executing the four designated releases.

Safety Considerations:

- Proper warm-up should precede the drill.
- Maintain a minimum distance of five-yards between each pair of paired drill participants.
- Helmets should be worn and chinstraps snapped.
- The coach should monitor closely the intensity of the drill.
- Instruct the defender not to *jam* the receiver in the head area.

Variations:

- Can be used as a form or live drill.
- Can be used simulating different down-and-distance situations.
- Can be used as a tight end release drill.

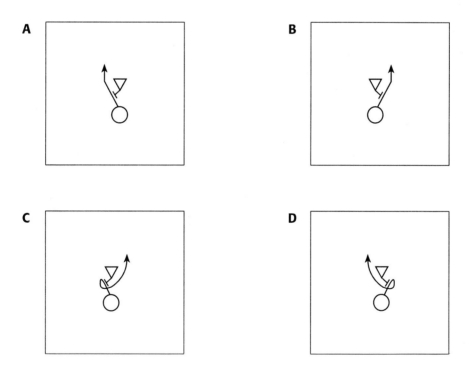

DRILL #35: STALK-BLOCKING DRILL

Dr. Gene A. Carpenter
Adams State College, Millersville University
Overall Record: 220-90-6

Objective: To teach and practice the proper fundamentals and techniques in the execution of the stalk block. Incorporated are skills of reaction and quickness.

Equipment Needed: Hand shield

Description:

- Align receivers in a straight line perpendicular to a selected line of scrimmage. The alignment should be relative to the offensive formation and such that the receivers are in the best position to block for the particular play called.
- A defender with a hand shield is positioned five yards in front of the first receiver.
- The coach stands behind the first receiver (see diagram).
- On the coach's cadence and snap count, the receiver drives out of his stance forcing the defender into his backpedal. The receiver works for a position one-yard outside the defender.
- The defender continues his retreat until the coach signals him to initiate his run support either straight ahead or to the outside.
- As the defender approaches the line of scrimmage, the receiver executes his stalk block.
- If the defender attacks straight-ahead (diagram A), the receiver must stop his penetration; and if he attacks to the outside (diagram B), the receiver drives him to the sideline.
- The drill continues until all the receivers have executed a sufficient number of stalk blocks.
- The drill should be conducted from both the left and right sides of the field and from left and right formations.

Coaching Points:

- Always check to see that the receivers are aligned correctly and are in their proper stances.
- Instruct the receivers to run-off the defender as far as possible.
- Make sure the receivers are under complete control as they execute their stalk blocks.

Safety Considerations:

- Proper warm-up is imperative with this drill.
- The drill area should be clear of all foreign articles.
- The drill should progress from form blocking to live blocking.
- The coach should monitor closely the intensity of the drill.
- Instruct the shield holder not to *jam* the receiver in the head area.

Variations:

- Can be used as a form or live-blocking drill.
- Can be used as a defensive back drill.

A
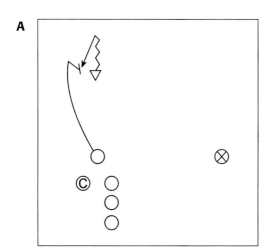

B
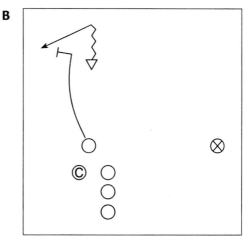

DRILL #36: SWIM-RELEASE DRILL

Don Nehlen
Bowling Green State University, West Virginia University
Overall Record: 202-112-6
National Coach of the Year: West Virginia 1988 and 1993
AFCA President: 1997

Objective: To teach and practice the proper fundamentals and techniques in the execution of a quick release off the line of scrimmage against a squat corner. Also incorporated are skills of driving out of a stance.

Equipment Needed: Cone, hand shield, and footballs

Description:

- Align wide receivers in a straight line behind a selected line of scrimmage. Their alignment should be in the proper relationship to the formation and the particular play to be run.
- A defensive squat corner with a hand shield lines up in his regular position six yards in front of the first receiver.
- A cone is placed six yards behind the defender.
- On the coach's cadence and snap count, the first wide receiver drives out of his stance and moves directly toward the squat corner.
- When reaching the corner, the receiver plants his release-side foot and punches the corner with the release-side hand. He then carries his opposite hand over the shoulder of the defender in a swimming motion as the inside leg crosses over and past the defender's hip.
- The receiver now completes the swim move and sprints to the cone.
- The drill continues until all the receivers have had a sufficient number of repetitions.
- The drill should be conducted from both the left and right sides of the field and from left and right formations.

Coaching Points:

- Always check to see that the receivers are aligned correctly and are in their proper stances.
- Insist that all the receivers drive out of their stances low and fast and without false stepping.

- Instruct the receivers to turn their shoulders as they execute the swim technique in an effort to reduce their hitting surface.
- Emphasize the importance of sprinting to the cone after the swim technique is executed.

Safety Considerations:

- It is imperative that proper warm-up precede this drill.
- The drill should progress from form to live work.
- The coach should monitor closely the intensity of the drill.
- Instruct the shield holder not to *jam* the receiver in the head area.

Variations:

- Can be used as a form or live drill.
- Can be used in teaching all pass routes.

DRILL #37: ACCURACY AND CONCENTRATION

Billy Joe
Cheyney State University, Central State University (OH), Florida A&M University
Overall Record: 221-89-4
National Champions: Central State 1990 and 1992
National Black College Champions: Central State 1983, 1984, 1985, 1986, 1987, 1988, 1989, 1990, 1991, and 1992; Florida A&M 1998
National Coach of the Year: Central State 1992
National Black College Coach of the Year: Central State 1986, 1987, 1988, 1989, and 1990; Florida A&M 1996
AFCA President: 1995

Objective: To teach and practice the proper mechanics of throwing the sideline pass with accuracy for the quarterback, and to teach and practice the proper sideline footwork, body control, and concentration while catching the football for wide receivers.

Equipment Needed: Footballs

Description:

- Align a wide receiver at the halfway point of his sideline pass route on a selected line of scrimmage (see diagram).

- Align a quarterback with a football in hand in the proper pass-drop relationship with the wide receiver. (Remember that the receiver's drill starting point is already halfway through his sideline-pass route.)

- Other drill participants stand adjacent to the drill area.

- On the quarterback's command, the wide receiver takes the last three steps of his downfield run, breaks for the sideline, and looks for the pass thrown by the quarterback.

- As the pass approaches, the receiver concentrates on catching the football and keeping his feet in bounds.

- The wide receiver coach is positioned in the catch area of the sidelines and monitors the catch.

- The drill continues until all the receivers have had a sufficient number of repetitions from both the left and the right sidelines.

Coaching Points:

- Make sure quarterbacks' pass drops are executed correctly.
- Make sure all quarterbacks practice the proper mechanics in throwing all passes.
- Instruct the quarterbacks to look off the receiver until his final drop step is made.
- Instruct the receivers to concentrate fully, maintain complete body control, catch the football with the hands, and to stay in bounds.

Safety Considerations:

- Full equipment should be worn.
- The drill area should be clear of all foreign articles. This includes the sideline areas.

Variation:

- Can be executed from the shotgun formation.

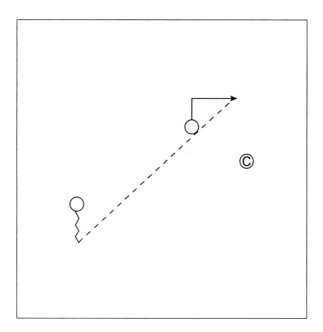

DRILL #38: FOCUS

> ## Joe Glenn
> Doane College, University of Northern Colorado, University of Montana
> Overall Record: 147-56-1
> National Champions: Northern Colorado 1996 and 1997; Montana 2001
> National Coach of the Year: Northern Colorado 1996 and 1997; Montana 2000

Objective: To teach and practice the proper fundamentals and techniques of catching the football. Incorporated are skills related to concentration and looking the ball into the hands.

Equipment Needed: Tennis balls or footballs

Description:

Phase I

- Align a row of wide receivers five yards from a designated sideline and behind a selected line of scrimmage (see diagram A).
- Position a quarterback (coach) on the rear hash mark with a tennis ball in hand and on the same line of scrimmage as the receiver.
- On the coach's cadence and snap count, the first wide receiver drives out of his stance and runs a one-half to three-quarter-speed fly pattern looking for the thrown tennis ball over his inside shoulder.
- The coach throws the tennis ball 10- to 15-yards downfield and the receiver catches the ball with two hands.
- The drill continues until all the wide receivers have had a sufficient number of repetitions catching the football from both the left and right sidelines.

Phase II

- Align a row of receivers in a straight line on a selected line of scrimmage and on the near numbers (see diagram B).
- Position a quarterback (coach) with a tennis ball in hand 15-yards downfield and 15-yards horizontal to the row of wide receivers.
- On the coach's cadence and snap count, the first receiver drives out of his stance and runs a one-half to three-quarter-speed crossing pattern and catches the tennis ball thrown by the coach.
- The drill continues until all the receivers have had a sufficient number of repetitions catching the tennis ball from both the left and the right.

Coaching Points:

- Always check to see that the wide receivers are in their proper stance.
- The coach should throw the tennis ball at game speed.
- Instruct the receivers to see their fingers catch the tennis ball.
- Insist that the receivers catch the tennis ball with the fingers of both hands.

Safety Considerations:

- Proper warm-up should precede the drill.
- The drill area should be clear of all foreign articles. This includes the sideline areas.
- Helmets should be worn and chinstraps snapped.
- Instruct the returning drill participants to stay clear of drill area. This includes the sideline area.

Variations:

- Can be performed using a football in place of the tennis ball.
- Can be used as a tight end drill.
- Can be used as a defensive back drill.

A 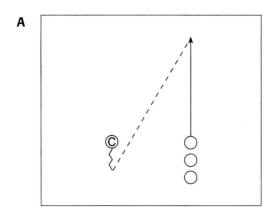 B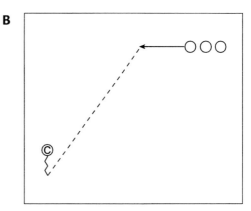

CHAPTER 6

Option-Offense

Drills

DRILL #39: OPTION DRILL

Roy Lee Kidd
Eastern Kentucky University
Overall Record: 307-119-8
National Champions: 1979 and 1982
National Coach of the Year: 1980 and 1981
AFCA President: 1998

Objective: To teach and practice the proper fundamentals and techniques in executing the handoff and pitch on the option play from the I formation.

Equipment Needed: Line-spacing strip, four cones, and footballs

Description:

- Place a line-spacing strip at the midpoint of a selected line of scrimmage.

- Cones are positioned on the line of scrimmage 10-yards outside the line-spacing strip. Additional cones are placed seven-yards downfield just inside each hash mark.

- Align a defensive end in his normal position.

- Position two quarterbacks side by side under centers at designated points on the line-spacing strip (see diagram). Three yards should separate the paired quarterbacks.

- A fullback and a tailback take an I-formation alignment relationship to the paired quarterback. (Tailback to the playside and fullback to the backside as shown in diagram.)

- Other offensive personnel stand behind the performing offensive players.

- On the backside quarterback's cadence, the centers snap the footballs. The backside quarterback executes a handoff to the fullback and continues down the line of scrimmage with his fake.

- The playside quarterback fakes to an imaginary fullback and then options the defensive end as he reacts to the play. The quarterback now pitches the football to the tailback or cuts and sprints upfield. The two cones, placed 10-yards outside the line-spacing strip, are used as an aiming point for the tailback's option course.

- Quarterbacks should alternate between backside and playside alignments.

- The drill continues until the alternating backfield has had a sufficient number of repetitions.

- The drill should be conducted from both left and right formations and from various field positions.

Coaching Points:

- Always check to see that all personnel are aligned correctly and are in their proper stances.
- Stress the importance of proper execution.
- Insist that the drill participants, with the exception of backside quarterbacks, sprint past the cones placed seven yards downfield.

Safety Considerations:

- Proper warm-up should precede the drill.
- The drill area should be clear of all foreign articles.
- Maintain a minimum distance of three yards between paired quarterbacks.

Variations:

- Can be used with a variety of option formations.
- Can incorporate other offensive and defensive personnel.

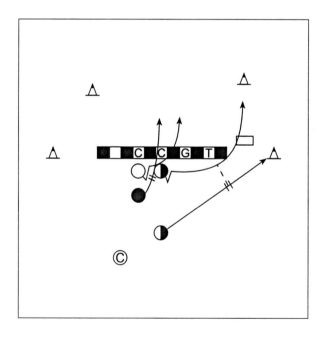

DRILL #40: CUT AND READ

Charles "Chuck" Broyles
Pittsburg State University
Overall Record: 123-23-2
National Champions: 1991
National Coach of the Year: 1991

Objective: To teach and practice the proper fundamentals and techniques in executing the inside handoff from the veer offense. Incorporated are skills related to running the correct mesh lane, receiving the handoff, making a full-speed north-south vertical cut for the running back, executing the inside-veer read and handoff, and accelerating to the pitch key for the quarterback.

Equipment Needed: Five large rubber trashcans, a hand shield, and footballs

Description:

- Position four rubber trashcans in a rectangular pattern approximately two- yards wide and three-yards deep adjacent to a selected line of scrimmage. A fifth trashcan is placed in the center of the rectangle (see diagram).

- Align a quarterback directly behind one of the front trashcans.

- Align a running back in his normal position, four-yards deep and head-up the center trashcan.

- Other drill participants stand behind the drill area.

- Position a coach, holding a hand shield, behind the center trashcan and another coach behind the opposite front trashcan.

- On his cadence and snap count, the quarterback moves to the veer mesh point with the running back. At the same time, the quarterback looks for a hand signal from the coach stepping from behind the opposite front trashcan. If he holds up one finger, the quarterback hands off to the running back. If he holds up two fingers, the quarterback will ride the running back, pull the football and accelerate to the pitch key while calling out the number of fingers held up by the coach.

- If the handoff is executed, the running back will react to the coach who is stepping from behind the middle trashcan by cutting in the opposite direction and sprinting through and past the two back trashcans.

- The drill continues until all the quarterbacks and running backs have had a sufficient number of repetitions from both left- and right-offensive alignments.

Coaching Points:

- Always check to see that the quarterbacks and running backs are aligned correctly and are in their proper stances.

- Stress the importance of proper executions.

- Insist that the drill be conducted at full speed.

- Make sure all the quarterbacks use the proper inside-veer footwork, reads and calls out the number signaled by the coach as they accelerate out of the handoff and to the pitch key.

- Make sure the running backs run their proper inside-veer path, form the proper handoff pocket, react correctly to the coach's stepping from behind the middle trashcan, and accelerate through and pass the back two trashcans.

- Instruct the running backs to use a *soft squeeze* on the football as they drive through the mesh point.

Safety Considerations:

- Proper warm-up should precede the drill.

- It is imperative that the coach standing behind the middle trashcan holds a hand shield in case of an accidental collision with the running back.

Variation:

- Can incorporate a third defender holding up a hand shield two-yards behind the rear trashcans and have the running back execute various moves such as a 360-degree spin or side step.

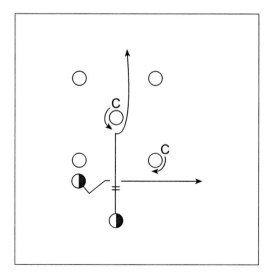

DRILL #41: PLAY PERFECTION – WIDENER'S DREAM PLAY

William B. "Bill" Manlove, Jr.
Widener University, Delaware Valley College, La Salle University
Overall Record: 212-110-1
National Champions: Widener 1977 and 1981
National Coach of the Year: Widener 1977 and 1981
AFCA President: 1991

Objective: To teach and practice the proper fundamentals in the execution of Widener's Dream Play—the outside veer. Incorporated are skills related to the center-quarterback ball exchange, blocking, and ballhandling.

Equipment Needed: Line-spacing strip, six hand shields, and footballs

Description:

- Place a line-spacing strip at the midpoint of a selected line of scrimmage.
- Position a noseguard, tackle, end, linebacker, strong safety, and cornerback in their normal positions. All defenders are holding hand shields.
- The offensive personnel (center, slot-side guard, tackle, split end, slot-back, quarterback, and running backs) break from the huddle and take their positions over the football.
- Other offensive personnel stand behind performing offensive players or serve as defensive players.
- On the quarterback's cadence and ball snap, the offense executes the outside veer as the defense reacts to the play.
- The drill continues until alternating offensives have had a sufficient number of repetitions.
- The drill should be conducted from both left and right formations and from various field positions.

Coaching Points:

- Always check to see that all personnel are aligned correctly and are in their proper stances.
- Make sure that center-quarterback exchange is executed property.
- Emphasize the importance of the entire offense driving off the ball as a unit.
- Instruct dive backs that it is imperative to run the dive lane hard and fast.
- Insist that all the defenders react to and give good resistance to blockers.

- The coach should signal the defensive end to close on the dive back, take the quarterback, or play pitch before each play.
- All coaching corrections should be made on the run and should not interfere with the tempo of the drill.

Safety Considerations:

- Proper warm-up should precede the drill.
- The drill area should be clear of all foreign articles.
- The drill should progress from formwork to live work.
- The coach should monitor closely the intensity of the drill.
- Instruct the defensive end not to be overly aggressive.
- When the drill is conducted live, the training staff should be placed on special alert.

Variations:

- Can be used as a form or live drill.
- Can be used with certain players designated as live performers such as the defensive end.
- Can be run to the tight end side.
- Can be used as a defensive drill.

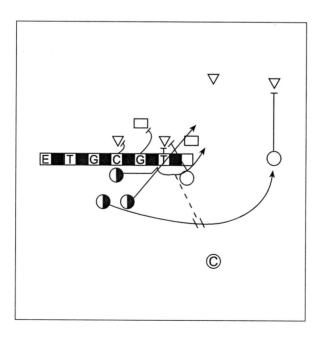

DRILL #42: TRIPLE-OPTION KEY DRILL

William F. "Bill" Yeoman
University of Houston
Overall Record: 160-108-8
College Football Hall of Fame: 2001

Objective: To teach and practice the proper fundamentals and techniques in the execution of the three-way option. Incorporated are skills of reading for the quarterbacks, running the correct *mesh* lane, and taking the handoff and pitch for the running backs.

Equipment Needed: Line-spacing strip, a hand shield, and footballs

Description:

- Place a line-spacing strip at the midpoint of a selected line of scrimmage.
- The coach, holding a hand shield, is positioned at either the defensive 4 or 5 technique.
- Alternating quarterbacks are placed at the 9 technique.
- The coach and the defensive end (quarterback) coordinate their defensive charge. (Coach and end slant in, coach and end slant out, and coach slants in and end slants out.)
- The offensive personnel (center, quarterback, fullback, and running backs) break the huddle and take their positions over the football.
- Other offensive backfields are positioned behind the performing offensive players.
- On the cadence and ball snap, the offense executes the three-way option as the defenders make their designated charges.
- The drill continues until the alternating backfields have had a sufficient number of repetitions.
- The drill should be conducted from both left and right formations and from various field positions.

Coaching Points:

- Always check to see that all personnel are aligned correctly and are in their proper stances.
- Instruct the defenders to execute their charges quickly and in a well-defined manner.

- Stress the importance of proper execution.
- Make sure the quarterbacks use the instructed techniques in executing the handoffs and pitches.
- After and only after quarterbacks have become comfortable with their reads, instruct defenders to play a little more *cat and mouse* with their charges.
- Insist that the drill be conducted at full speed.
- The coach should designate defensive charges that allow different quarterbacks to work on their particular weaknesses such as the handoff, quarterback keep, or pitch.

Safety Considerations:

- Proper warm-up should precede the drill.
- The drill area should be clear of all foreign articles.
- It is imperative that the coach, standing at the 4 or 5 technique, holds a hand shield in case of a collision with the dive back.

Variations:

- Can use with the two-way option (outside veer) by moving the coach to the 9 technique and other defender to the strong safety position.
- Can be used in attacking the split end side.

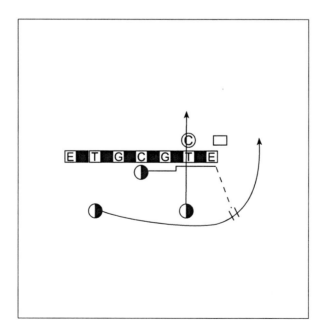

DRILL #43: RIDE AND DECIDE

Fisher DeBerry
United States Air Force Academy
Overall Record: 141-78-1
National Coach of the Year: 1985
Fellowship of Christian Athletes Grant Teaff Coach of the Year: 1998
AFCA President: 1996

Objective: To teach and practice the proper fundamental and techniques in the execution of the triple-option versus a seven-man front. Special emphasis is placed on the quarterback making his first and second read under pressure.

Equipment Needed: Football

Description:

- Align a defensive tackle and a defensive end in their normal seven-man front alignment on a selected line of scrimmage.

- Position a quarterback, a fullback, and a pitch back in their normal triple-option alignment over the defense.

- Alternating offensive backfields stand behind the performing offensive players.

- On the quarterback's cadence and snap count, the backfield executes the triple-option as defenders execute a variety of designated charges.

- If the defensive tackle and the defensive end both run a *hot stunt* (see diagram A), the quarterback should pull the football, take a drop step, stop and pitch the football to the pitch back.

- If the defensive tackle closes on the fullback and the defensive end slow plays the quarterback, the quarterback should pull the football and attack the defensive end by dipping the shoulders to the inside to draw his tackle. The quarterback then pitches the football to the pitch back (see diagram B).

- If the defensive tackle drives up the field to take the quarterback, the quarterback should hand the football to the fullback (see diagram C).

- The drill continues until all the backfield personnel have had a sufficient number of repetitions from both left and right formations and from various field positions.

Coaching Points:

- Always check to see that the backfield personnel are aligned correctly and are in their proper stances.

- Stress the importance of proper execution.
- Insist that the drill be conducted at full speed.
- Instruct the backfield personnel to always take their designated option paths.

Safety Considerations:

- Proper warm-up should precede the drill.
- The drill area should be clear of all foreign articles.
- The drill should progress from formwork to full speed.
- The coach should monitor closely the intensity of the drill.

Variation:

- Can be used in executing the triple option against an eight-man front.

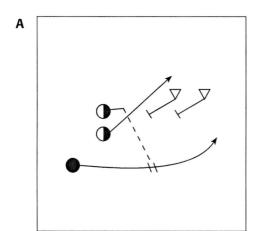

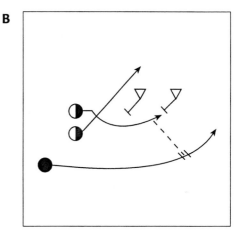

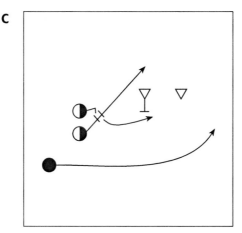

DRILL #44: TRIPLE OPTION

Frank Solich
University of Nebraska
Overall Record: 42-9-0

Objective: To teach and practice the proper fundamentals and technique in executing the triple option from the I formation.

Equipment Needed: Line spacing strip, a hand shield, and footballs

Description:

- Place a line-spacing strip at the midpoint of a selected line of scrimmage.
- Align a backfield in the proper triple-option I formation behind the line-spacing strip.
- Position the running back coach, holding a hand shield, at the defensive tackle position and the quarterback coach at the defensive end position.
- Other offensive backfields stand behind the performing offensive backfield.
- On the quarterback's cadence and snap count, the I-formation backfield executes the triple option as the defenders (coaches) execute their designated charges.
- If the defensive tackle (coach) closes on the fullback, the quarterback pulls the football and proceeds to the pitch read. If the defensive tackle (coach) maintains his width, the quarterback hands the football to the fullback.
- If the defensive end (quarterbacks coach) closes on the quarterback, he pitches the football to the I back. If the defensive end (coach) maintains his width, the quarterback keeps the football and sprints up the field.
- The drill continues until the I-back personnel have had a sufficient number of repetitions from both the left and right formations and from various field alignments.

Coaching Points:

- Always check to see that the I backfields are aligned correctly and that all the drill participants are in their proper stances.
- Stress the importance of proper execution.
- Insist that the drill be conducted at full speed.
- Instruct all the backfield personnel as to their designated option paths.
- The coach should monitor closely the quarterbacks' read and handoff in the mesh lane and the I backs' pitch relationship with the quarterbacks.

- Instruct the quarterbacks to take a 45-degree angle step and extend the football back toward the fullback while he reads the charges of the defensive tackle and defensive end to determine if he should hand off to the fullbacks or pull the football and execute his second option.

- In reading the dive, the quarterbacks should place the ball in the fullbacks' pocket at the numbers and ride the fullback as they read the defensive tackle.

- Instruct the I backs to read the charge of the defensive end, and if the end attacks the quarterback, they should *throttle down* so they can maintain the proper pitch relationship with the quarterback.

- Instruct the quarterbacks that if the defensive tackle closes and the defensive end slow plays the pitch, the quarterback must pull the football from the fullback and attack the defensive end as the second option is executed.

Safety Considerations:

- Proper warm-up should precede the drill.
- The drill area should be clear of all foreign articles.
- It is imperative that the coach aligned at the dive read holds a hand shield in case of an accidental collision with the fullback.

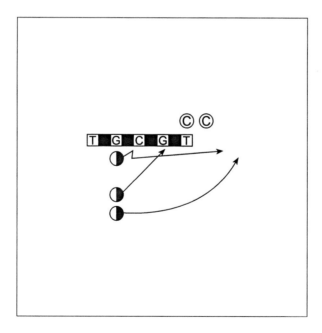

DRILL #45: TAPE

Kenneth "Ken" Sparks
Carson-Newman College
Overall Record: 211-51-2
National Champions: 1983, 1984, 1986, 1988, and 1989
National Coach of the Year: 1984
Fellowship of Christian Athletes Grant Teaff Coach of the Year: 1999

Objective: To teach and practice the proper fundamentals and techniques in executing the inside handoff from the veer offense. Incorporated are skills related to running the correct veer lane for the running backs and reading the *no-mesh* option for the quarterbacks.

Equipment Needed: One large block dummy, a hand shield, and footballs

Description:

- Align a veer backfield on a selected line of scrimmage.

- Place a large block dummy behind the line of scrimmage and at a 45-degree angle adjacent to the quarterback (see diagram).

- Align two coaches, one holding a hand shield at the dive read position and the other at the pitch read position. A player or manager is aligned at the offensive tackle position.

- Other drill participants stand behind the performing offensive players.

- On his cadence and snap count, the quarterback steps into the line of scrimmage avoiding the block dummy and points the football at the dive-read defender (coach).

- The running back drives to the outside leg of the offensive guard and *brushes* the tail of the offensive tackle (player or manager) that is blocking down to the inside.

- The quarterback reads the dive defender's (coach's) charge and either hand the football to the running back or proceeds to and executes the pitch read against the pitch defender (coach).

- The drill continues until all the drill participants have had a sufficient number of repetitions from both left and right formations.

Coaching Points:

- Always check to see that all the drill participants are aligned correctly and are in their proper stances.

- Stress the importance of proper execution.
- Insist that the drill be conducted at full speed.
- Instruct the dive-and-pitch defenders to present the quarterbacks with various reads.
- Instruct the quarterbacks to always point the football at the dive read defender, and if the dive read defender comes to take the football, he should pull the football and proceed to the pitch read.
- Instruct the pitch back to always maintain the proper pitch relationship to the quarterback.

Safety Considerations:

- Proper warm-up should precede the drill.
- The drill area should be clear of all foreign articles.
- It is imperative that the coach positioned at the dive read hold a hand shield in case of an accidental collision with the dive back.

Variation:

- Can be used in the execution of the two-way option, the counter option, and the mid-line option.

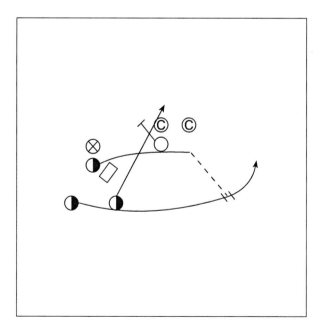

CHAPTER 7

Passing Game

Drills

DRILL #46: MAXIMUM-PASS DRILL

Phillip James "Jim" Butterfield
Ithaca College
Overall Record: 206-71-1
National Champions: 1979, 1988, and 1991
National Coach of the Year: 1988 and 1991
College Football Hall of Fame: 1997

Objective: To teach and practice the proper fundamentals and techniques in the execution of various pass patterns.

Equipment Needed: Footballs

Description:

- Align three quarterbacks (A, B, C) under centers at the midpoint of a selected line of scrimmage. A four-foot separation is between the centers.

- Position four receivers at various alignments on the line of scrimmage. Each receiver must be positioned at an appropriate distance relative to the quarterback who will pass him the football and the pattern to be run (see diagram).

- Coaches align themselves as defenders.

- With the middle quarterback designated to call cadence, quarterbacks execute one of three pass drop actions (quarterback A—a three-step quick pass, quarterback B —a play-action pass, and quarterback C—a sprint-out pass).

- Alternating drill participants stand adjacent to the drill area.

- On the cadence and ball snap, the quarterbacks take their designated pass drops and pass the footballs to assigned receivers who have run predetermined pass routes.

- The drill continues until the quarterbacks and receivers have run a sufficient number of varying pass actions and patterns.

- The drill should be conducted from both left and right formations and from various field positions.

Coaching Points:

- Always check to see that all personnel are aligned correctly and are in proper stances.

- Instruct the quarterbacks to rotate their positions under the centers after each pass.

- Coaches should present imaginary secondary reads for quarterbacks and receivers.

- Make sure all quarterbacks practice the proper mechanics in throwing all passes.
- Make sure all quarterbacks take their proper pass drop action.
- Instruct all receivers to run all their patterns correctly and with authority.
- Insist that the drill be conducted at full speed.

Safety Considerations:

- Proper warm-up should precede the drill.
- The drill area should be clear of all foreign articles.
- Instruct the receivers to run complementary pass patterns.
- Maintain a minimum distance of four-yards between the three quarterbacks.
- All quarterback pass-drop actions must always be in the same direction.

Variations:

- Can be used with all quarterbacks taking the same pass-drop action.
- Can be used with receivers running a variety of complementing patterns.
- Can be used with coaches or secondary personnel providing reads for quarterbacks.
- Can incorporate offensive backs and run play-action passes.
- Can be used as a secondary drill.

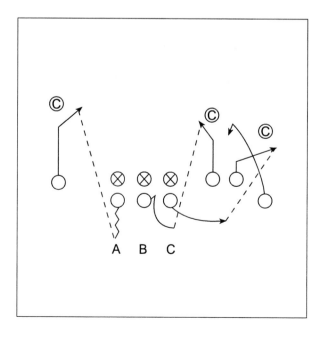

DRILL #47: CURL READ

Larry Kehres
Mount Union College
Overall Record: 178-17-3
National Champions: 1993, 1996, 1997, 1998, 2000, and 2001
National Coach of the Year 1993, 1996, 1997, 1998, 2000, and 2001

Objective: To teach and practice the proper mechanics of passing the football and reading the open receiver against a curl/flat defender for quarterbacks; running the correct pass route and catching the football for the receivers.

Equipment Needed: Footballs

Description:

- Align a quarterback and center over the football at the midpoint of a selected line of scrimmage.
- Position twin receivers in their proper curl/flat-pass play relationship to the quarterback.
- Other drill participants stand adjacent to the drill area.
- A defender (coach) is positioned at the curl/flat defender position.
- On the quarterback's cadence and snap count, the receivers run their designated curl/flat-pass routes as the quarterback takes his normal five-step pass drop (see diagram).
- As the quarterback is completing his pass drop, the defender (coach) moves to cover either the curl or flat receiver. (Movement by the coach is only two steps.) The quarterback reads the coverage of the defender (coach) and passes to the open receiver.
- The drill continues until all participants have had a sufficient number of executions.
- The drill should be conducted from various field alignments and from both left and right formations.

Coaching Points:

- Always check to see that all the drill participants are aligned correctly and are in their proper stances.
- Instruct the quarterbacks to make their read on the defender (coach) as they take their fifth drop step.
- Insist that the receivers run their curl/flat-pass routes correctly and at full speed.

- Make sure all quarterbacks use proper passing mechanics with each pass thrown.
- Insist that the receivers catch the football with their hands, tuck it away, and sprint for a designated distance.

Safety Considerations:

- Proper warm-up should precede the drill.
- The drill area should be cleared of all foreign articles. This includes the sideline areas.
- Helmets should be worn and chinstraps snapped.

Variations:

- Can be used with any combination-pass patterns.
- Can be used with a three-receiver pass route utilizing three defenders.

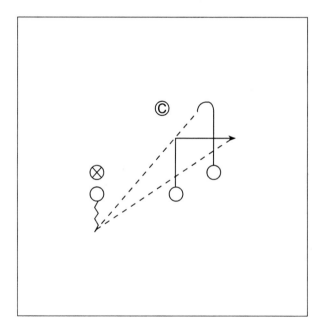

DRILL #48: RELAY-LINE DRILL

Darrell Eugene Mudra
Adams State University, North Dakota State University, Montreal Alouettes,
Western Illinois University, Florida State University,
Eastern Illinois University, University of Northern Iowa
Overall Record: 200-81-4
National Champions: North Dakota State 1965; Eastern Illinois 1978
College Football Hall of Fame: 2000

Objective: To teach and practice the proper fundamentals and techniques in throwing and catching the football from various receiver-quarterback relationships. Can also be used as a warm-up drill.

Equipment Needed: Footballs

Description:

- Position all receivers and quarterbacks into two groups on selected yard lines as shown in diagram. Twenty yards should separate the two groups.

- Align each group in a receiver-quarterback relationship that allows receiver to make an over-the-shoulder catch as shown in diagram A.

- On quarterback's cadence, the first receiver in each group runs across the field as the respective quarterback passes him the football.

- After the catch is made, each receiver carries the football to the quarterback in the other group and joins that group.

- After all the drill participants have had a sufficient number of repetitions from this alignment, the quarterbacks change their positions to set up a crossing-pattern relationship with receivers (see diagram B).

- The drill continues until all the drill participants have had a sufficient number of repetitions.

Coaching Points:

- Make sure all the quarterbacks practice the proper mechanics in throwing all passes.

- Insist that receivers catch all passes with their hands.

- Instruct receivers to place special emphasis on concentration.

Safety Considerations:

- The drill area should be clear of all foreign articles.
- The drill should progress from half speed with short passes to full speed with longer passes.
- Helmets should be worn with chinstraps snapped.

Variations:

- Can be used with quarterback and receivers aligned in a variety of relationships.
- Can be used with receivers running in a counterclockwise direction.

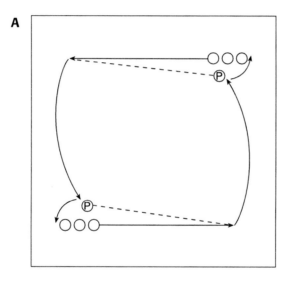

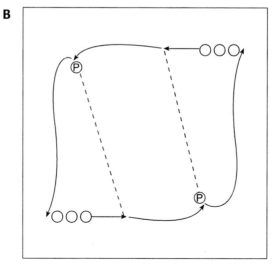

DRILL #49: SCRAMBLE DRILL

John T. Majors
Iowa State University, University of Pittsburgh, University of Tennessee
Overall Record: 185-137-10
National Champions: Pittsburgh 1976
National Coach of the Year: Pittsburgh 1973 and 1976
AFCA President: 1990

Objective: To teach and practice skills related to scramble-passing and pass- receiving rules. Incorporated are skills related to throwing the football while being chased, finding the open receiver, throwing the ball away if necessary for the quarterback, and redirecting a called pass pattern by the receiver.

Equipment Needed: Footballs

Description:

- Align a skeleton-pass offense over the football at the midpoint of a selected line of scrimmage.

- A perimeter-pass defense is positioned over the offense. Two additional defenders are placed at the defensive guard position.

- Alternating offensive personnel stand adjacent to their drill areas.

- The quarterback instructs all offensive personnel as to the pass pattern to be run using the regular audible system.

- On the cadence and ball snap, the quarterback executes his pass drop as the receivers run their assigned pass routes.

- The defensive-perimeter players react to the offense in any manner they wish. Their goal is to intercept or prevent the reception. The two additional defenders (guards) are instructed to delay their charge until the quarterback has initiated his scramble. They then take chase and tag the quarterback.

- When the quarterback initiates his scramble, the receivers alter their designated pass route and follow their normal scramble rules (see diagram).

- The drill continues until the alternating personnel have had a sufficient number of repetitions.

- The drill should be conducted from both left and right formations and from various field positions.

Coaching Points:

- Always check to see that all personnel are aligned correctly and are in their proper stances.
- Make sure all the receivers follow their assigned scramble rules.
- Instruct the quarterbacks to tuck the football and run or throw the pass away if necessary.
- Make sure all the receivers sprint to the football and become blockers after the pass is thrown.
- Insist that the drill be conducted at full speed.

Safety Considerations:

- Proper warm-up is imperative with this drill.
- The drill area should be clear of all foreign articles. This includes the sideline areas.
- Although the drill is conducted at full speed, the tackling of receivers is not encouraged except under the most monitored conditions.
- The coach should monitor closely the intensity of the drill.
- A quick whistle is imperative with this drill.

Variations:

- Can have the quarterback reverse his field after his initial scramble.
- Can be used as a defensive drill.

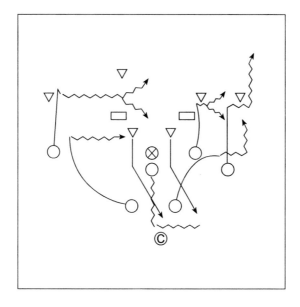

DRILL #50: PLAY-ROUTE REPETITION

Lee J. Tressel (Deceased)
[Drill submitted by Dick Tressel]
Baldwin-Wallace College
Overall Record: 155-52-6
National Champions: 1978
National Coach of the Year: 1978
College Football Hall of Fame: 1996

Objective: To teach and practice the proper mechanics of setting up and passing the football for quarterbacks, and running the correct pass route and catching the football for receivers.

Equipment Needed: 10 footballs

Description:

- Select a designated pass play to be used as the *pass play of the day*.

- Align five quarterbacks (with two footballs each) on the hash marks on the right side of the field, and on selected lines of scrimmage as noted in the following bulleted procedures four through eight. (All quarterbacks are positioned on the same side of the field hash marks.) Quarterbacks one, two, and four throw passes toward midfield, while quarterbacks three and five throw passes toward the end zone (see diagram).

- Quarterback number one positions himself on the hash mark of his own goal line and passes the football to the flankers.

- Quarterback number two positions himself on the hash mark of his own 15-yard line and passes the football to the tight ends.

- Quarterback number three positions himself on the hash mark of the opponent's 16-yard line and passes the football to the split ends.

- Quarterback number four positions himself on the hash mark of his own 35-yard line and passes the football to the strongside running backs.

- Quarterback number five positions himself on the hash mark on the opponent's 36-yard line and passes the football to the weakside running backs.

- On the individual quarterback's cadence and snap count, receivers run their designated *pass-play-of-the-day* pass routes as quarterbacks execute their correct pass drops. Each quarterback throws two passes from each field alignment and then moves upfield to the next field alignment. The quarterback passing to the weakside running backs proceeds to the goal line.

- All the receivers remain at the same field alignment throughout the drill. They are also responsible for returning the footballs to the quarterback at their station.
- After each quarterback has thrown two passes from each field alignment, the passing field is reversed and quarterbacks and receivers move to the opposite hash mark and the drill continues.

Coaching Points:

- Always check to see that all the drill participants are aligned correctly and are in their proper stances.
- Stress the importance of running all pass routes correctly and at full speed.
- Instruct all quarterbacks to follow their read progression with every pass. (Each quarterback will assume a specific coverage before calling the cadence.)
- Make sure the quarterbacks take the correct pass drop and use proper passing mechanics with each thrown pass.
- Insist that the quarterbacks hustle as they move from one station to another and that the receivers sprint downfield after each catch and hustle as they return the ball to the quarterback.

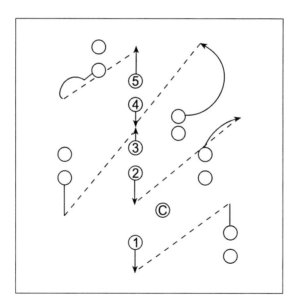

Safety Considerations:

- Proper warm-up should precede the drill.
- The drill area should be clear of all foreign objects. This includes the sideline areas.
- Insist that alternating pass receivers remain alert and align themselves in a safe position as pass patterns are being thrown.
- In assigning receivers to each station, the coach much be fully aware of each pass route to be run and the field allotment needed.

PART II
DEFENSIVE DRILLS

CHAPTER 8

Defensive Back

Drills

DRILL #51: BACKPEDAL PROGRAM

Vincent J. "Vince" Dooley
University of Georgia
Overall Record: 201-77-10
National Champions: 1980
National Coach of the Year: 1980 and 1982
College Football Hall of Fame: 1994
Amos Alonzo Stagg Award: 2001
AFCA President: 1985

Objective: To teach and practice the proper fundamentals in executing the backpedal. Incorporated are skills related to agility, reaction, and acceleration.

Equipment Needed: Football

Description:

- Align two defensive backs 10-yards apart across from a selected line of scrimmage.
- The coach, holding a football, is positioned in between the defenders on the line of scrimmage.
- Other defensive backs stand adjacent to the drill area.
- The drill is conducted in seven phases as follows:
  - *Back and forth.* On the coach's command, the defensive backs drive from their stances and backpedal for five yards and then push forward for five yards. Procedure is repeated ten times (see diagram A).
  - *Backpedal: come straight back to front.* On the coach's command, the defensive backs drive from their stances and backpedal for 10 yards and then push off the back foot and sprint back to their original positions. Procedure is repeated five or six times, alternating pushing off the left and right foot (see diagram B).
  - *Backpedal: push right or left.* On the coach's command, the defensive backs drive from their stances and backpedal for 10 yards and then cut and sprint 10 yards at a 90-degree angle. Procedure is repeated five times with the defensive backs sprinting both left and right (see diagram C).
  - *Backpedal: push up and in at a 45-degree angle.* On the coach's command, the defensive backs drive from their stances and backpedal for 10 yards and then cut and sprint 10 yards at 45-degree angles toward the line of scrimmage. Procedure is repeated five times with the defensive backs sprinting at 45-degree angles both left and right (see diagram D).

- *Backpedal: turn and break deep at a 45-degree angle.* On the coach's command, the defensive backs drive from their stances and backpedal for 10 yards and then cut and sprint 10 yards at 45-degree angles away from the line of scrimmage. Procedure is repeated five times with the defensive backs sprinting at 45-degree angles both left and right (see diagram E).
- *Backpedal: turn deep at a 45-degree angle; roll around on deep throw back.* On the coach's command, the preceding procedure is repeated. However, after the ten-yard 45-degree angle sprint away from the line of scrimmage, the defensive backs turn completely around with their backs away from the line of scrimmage and sprint back at 45-degree angles. Procedure is repeated five times with the defensive backs turning and sprinting both left and right (see diagram F).
- *Backpedal for speed.* On the coach's command, the defensive backs backpedal for speed at distances of 10 yards, 20 yards, and 40 yards. Procedure is repeated five times at each distance.

Coaching Points:

- Always check to see that the defensive backs are in their proper stances.
- Instruct the defensive backs to keep a base of six to eight inches with their toes pointing straight ahead as they execute all backpedals.
- Insist that the defensive backs maintain a low center of gravity with the weight on the front foot. Heels should never touch the ground.
- Make sure the defensive backs keep their head up throughout the drill.
- Emphasize that all breaks off the backpedals should coincide with a particular pass pattern to be covered (out, curl, flag, post, etc.).
- Insist that the drill be conducted at full speed.

Safety Considerations:

- Proper warm-up should precede the drill with particular emphasis on the lower back, hamstrings, and groin.
- The drill area should be clear of all foreign articles.
- Maintain a minimum distance of 10-yards between performing drill participants.

Variation:

- Can be used with the coach executing a pass drop and throwing passes.

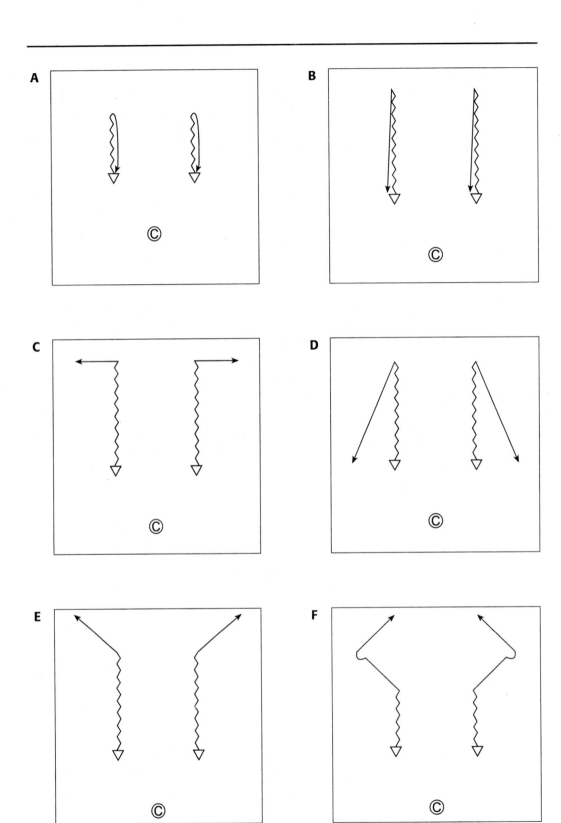

DRILL #52: BALL-REACTION DRILL

John H. Cooper
University of Tulsa, Arizona State University, The Ohio State University
Overall Record: 193-83-6
National Coach of the Year: Arizona State 1986
AFCA President: 1992

Objective: To teach and practice the proper fundamentals and techniques of breaking on and intercepting a pass. Incorporated are skills related to agility and quickness.

Equipment Needed: Footballs

Description:

- Align a row of defensive backs 25-yards downfield from the midpoint of a selected line of scrimmage.

- A quarterback (coach) stands in front of the defensive backs and on the line of scrimmage.

- A row of receivers is placed perpendicular to the line of scrimmage and 10-yards away and on both sides of the coach (see diagram).

- On the coach's command, the first wide receiver in each line runs a post pattern.

- The first defensive back reads the quarterback (coach) and breaks on and intercepts the thrown pass. He then tucks the football away and sprints to the coach and hands it to him.

- The drill continues until all the defensive backs have had a sufficient number of repetitions.

Coaching Points:

- Always check to see that the defensive backs are aligned correctly and are in their proper stances.

- Instruct the defensive backs to always break in front of the receivers and to intercept the football at its highest point.

- Instruct the receivers that they are not to make the reception but can harass the defender by yelling or faking a tackle.

- Insist that the drill be conducted at full speed.

Safety Considerations:

- Proper warm-up should precede the drill.
- The drill area should be clear of all foreign articles.
- Under no circumstances should this be a contact drill.
- The coach should time his pass to ensure that there is no danger of the receivers running into each other.

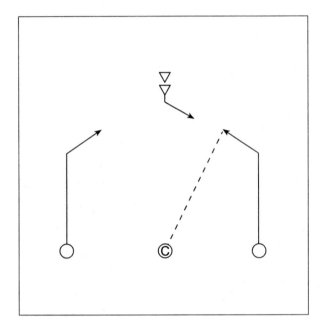

DRILL #53: CONFIDENCE DRILL

Carmen "Carm" Cozza
Yale University
Overall Record: 179-119-5
College Football Hall of Fame: 2002
AFCA President: 1978

Objective: To teach and practice the proper fundamentals and techniques of covering the three-deep pass zone and intercepting a pass.

Equipment Needed: Footballs

Description:

- Position four rows of receivers at equal distances across the field on a selected line of scrimmage (see diagram).
- A three-deep secondary is aligned in its normal position over the receivers.
- The quarterback (coach), holding a football, is positioned at the midpoint of the line of scrimmage.
- Alternating defensive units are positioned on the sideline.
- On the cadence and snap count, the coach executes his pass drop as the first receiver in each row sprints straight downfield.
- The coach fakes one way and then passes the football to any one of the receivers as the defensive backs break for the interception.
- The drill continues until all the defensive backs have had a sufficient number of repetitions.

Coaching Points:

- Always check to see that the defensive backs are aligned correctly and are in their proper stances.
- Make sure the defensive backs keep both the receivers and the quarterback in their field of vision.
- Insist that the defensive backs always remain in their proper pass coverage zones.
- Instruct defensive backs always to intercept a pass at its highest point.

Safety Considerations:

- Proper warm-up should precede the drill.

- The drill area should be clear of all foreign articles.
- Instruct the receivers to always remain in their designated running lanes and to avoid all contact with the defensive backs.

Variations:

- Can be used with various quarterback-pass drops.
- Can be used with receivers running various coordinated patterns.
- Can incorporate linebackers.

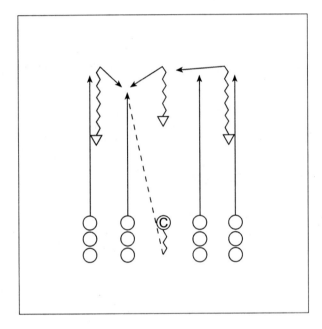

DRILL #54: CUSHION DRILL

T C. "Chan" Gailey
Samford University, Troy State University, Birmingham Fire,
Dallas Cowboys, Georgia Institute of Technology
Overall Record: 54-36-1
National Champions: Troy State 1984
National Coach of the Year: Troy State 1984

Objective: To teach and practice the proper fundamentals and techniques of cushioning a receiver. Can also be used as a warm-up drill.

Equipment Needed: None

Description:

- Position a row of wide receivers perpendicular to a selected line of scrimmage.
- Align a defensive back in his normal position across from the first wide receiver.
- Other defensive backs stand adjacent to the drill area.
- The coach will vary his position around the drill area.
- On the coach's command, the first receiver runs one-half to three-quarter speed straight down the field. The defensive back backpedals, keeping a designated cushion of two-yards vertical and one-yard horizontal on either the inside or outside of the receiver. If the wide receiver breaks the designated cushion, then the defensive back will have to turn out of his backpedal and run with the receiver.
- The drill continues until all the defensive backs have had a sufficient number of repetitions both to the inside and outside of the receiver.

Coaching Points:

- Always check to see that the defensive backs are aligned correctly and are in their proper stances.
- Insist that the defensive backs execute their backpedal correctly.
- The coach should view the drill from various angles in order to check for the proper vertical and horizontal cushion.

Safety Considerations:

- Proper warm-up should precede the drill.
- The drill area should be clear of all foreign articles.

Variations:

- Can be used with receivers cutting left and right as they run downfield.
- Can be used with receivers running at full speed.
- Can be used with a quarterback throwing a pass to the receivers.

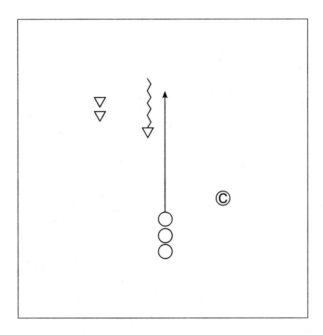

DRILL #55: FOUR-POINT BREAKING DRILL

Frank M. Beamer
Murray State University, Virginia Polytechnic Institute
Overall Record: 149-88-4
National Coach of the Year: Virginia Tech 1999

Objective: To teach and practice the proper fundamentals and techniques of breaking on and intercepting the football.

Equipment Needed: Four large blocking dummies and footballs

Description:

- Position a defensive back at the midpoint of a selected yard line.
- The quarterback (coach), holding a football, stands 20 yards in front of the defensive back.
- Other defensive backs stand adjacent to the drill area.
- A dummy is placed 10 yards on both sides of the defensive back. Two additional dummies are placed 20-yards downfield and 30-yards apart (see diagram).
- On the coach's signal, the defensive back initiates his backpedal. When the defensive back has backpedaled approximately five yards, the coach will turn and throw the football (with long arm motion) to one of the four dummies.
- The defensive back reads the long arm motion of the quarterback and sprints to the football and makes the interception.
- The drill continues until all the defensive backs have had a sufficient number of repetitions.

Coaching Points:

- Check to see that the defensive backs are in their proper stances.
- Insist that the defensive backs execute their backpedal correctly keeping their eyes on the quarterback.
- Instruct the defensive backs to get a good plant off their backpedal and to take the proper angle to intercept the football.
- Make sure the defensive backs break through or in front of the dummy as they intercept the pass at its highest point.

Safety Considerations:

- Proper warm-up should precede the drill.
- The drill area should be clear of all foreign articles.

Variations:

- Can be used with dummies placed at varying positions on the field.
- Can be used as a linebacker drill.

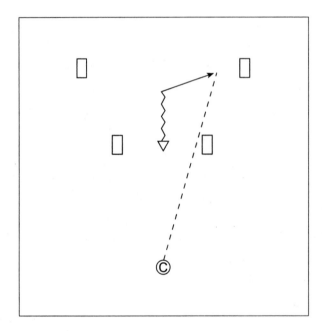

DRILL #56: INTERCEPTION DRILL

Don E. James
Kent State University, University of Washington
Overall Record: 178-76-3
National Champions: Washington 1991
National Coach of the Year: Washington 1977 and 1991
College Football Hall of Fame: 1997
AFCA President: 1989

Objective: To teach and practice the proper fundamentals and techniques of breaking on and intercepting the football. Incorporated are skills related to the backpedal, the plant, and the angle to take to a thrown pass.

Equipment Needed: Footballs

Description:

- Position two defensive backs five-yards apart at the midpoint of a selected line of scrimmage.
- The coach, holding a football, stands 10 yards in front of the defensive backs. The coach designates a receiver and defender.
- Other defensive backs stand adjacent to the drill area.
- On the coach's signal (shows pass), both defensive backs initiate their backpedal.
- When the defensive backs have backpedaled the desired distance, the coach will turn his shoulders and throw the football to the designated receiver.
- The designated defender reads the coach's shoulder turn and release, and then plants and breaks for the interception.
- The drill continues until all the defensive backs have had a sufficient number of repetitions.

Coaching Points:

- Always check to see that the defensive backs are in their proper stances.
- Insist that the defensive backs execute their backpedal correctly.
- Instruct the defensive backs to get a good plant off their backpedal and to take the proper angle to intercept the football.
- Make sure the defensive backs break in front of the receiver as they intercept the pass at its highest point.

Safety Considerations:

- It is imperative that proper warm-up precede this drill.
- The defenders should be instructed to drive in front of the receiver and not into him.
- The coach should monitor closely the intensity of the drill.

Variations:

- Can be used with varying distances between the two defensive backs and between the defensive backs and the coach. (The defensive backs can be 10-yards apart and 15 yards from the coach, or the defensive backs can be 15-yards apart and 20 yards from the coach.)
- Can be used with one defensive back positioned five-yards deeper than the other.
- Can be used without designating a receiver.
- Can be used as a linebacker drill.

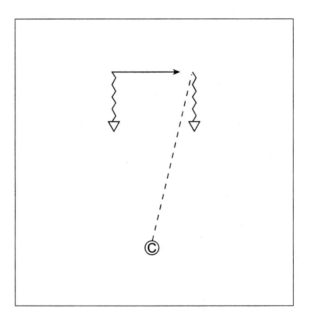

DRILL #57: SIDELINE-TACKLING DRILL

Barry L. Switzer
University of Oklahoma, Dallas Cowboys
Overall Record: 202-55-8
National Champions: 1974, 1975, and 1985
Super Bowl XXX Champions
College Football Hall of Fame: 2001

Objective: To teach and practice the proper fundamentals and techniques in executing a sideline tackle.

Equipment Needed: Scrimmage vest (optional) and footballs

Description:

- Position a row of defensive backs on the hash mark and perpendicular to a selected yard line.
- Align a row of ballcarriers 10-yards away from and facing the defensive backs.
- The coach, holding a football, stands in a quarterback pitch relationship to the ballcarriers.
- On command, the coach pitches the football to the first ballcarrier, who runs upfield between the hash marks and sideline.
- The defensive back reads run, initiates his backpedal back and to the outside, and then sprints to an inside-out position on the ballcarrier forcing him to the sideline.
- If the ballcarrier should cut back, the defensive back executes a shoulder tackle. If the ballcarrier continues on his outside path, the defensive back drives him out of bounds.
- The drill continues until all the defensive backs have had a sufficient number of repetitions.
- The drill should be conducted both left and right.

Coaching Points:

- Always check to see that the defensive backs are aligned correctly and are in their proper stances.
- Instruct the tacklers to always maintain an inside-out leverage on the ballcarrier.
- Make sure defensive backs practice proper fundamentals and techniques of safe tackling.

Safety Considerations:

- It is imperative that proper warm-up precede this drill.
- The drill area should be clear of all foreign articles. This includes the sideline areas.
- The drill should progress from form tackling to live tackling.
- The coach should monitor closely the intensity of the drill.
- The coach should watch for and eliminate all unacceptable matchups as to size and athletic ability.
- Instruct all defensive backs as to the proper fundamentals and techniques of safe tackling.
- The training staff should be placed on special alert.

Variations:

- Can be used as a form or live tackling drill.
- Can be used as an offensive back drill.
- Can be used as a defensive end and linebacker drill.

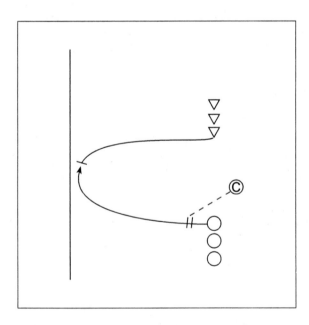

DRILL #58: TACKLE-AND-PURSUIT DRILL

George T. Welsh
United States Naval Academy, University of Virginia
Overall Record: 190-133-4
National Coach of the Year: Virginia 1989, 1991, and 1998

Objective: To teach and practice the proper fundamentals and techniques of pursuit and sideline tackling.

Equipment Needed: Six cones and footballs

Description:

- Align two rows of ballcarriers three-yards apart and perpendicular to a selected line of scrimmage. The first two ballcarriers hold footballs.

- Place three cones to form a 15-yard equilateral triangle on each side of the two rows of ballcarriers. The base of the triangle is placed on the selected line of scrimmage. The bases of the two triangles are also 15-yards apart. (See diagram)

- Position a row of defensive backs two yards off the line of scrimmage and facing the two rows of ballcarriers.

- The coach stands behind the defensive backs and signals one ballcarrier to run straight ahead, and the other to circle behind the apex of the triangle and to proceed upfield.

- On the coach's command, the designated ballcarrier runs straight ahead and the defensive back reacts and executes a form tackle. The tackler holds the form tackle until the coach blows his whistle.

- When the coach blows his whistle, the tackler releases the first ballcarrier and pursues and form tackles the second ballcarrier who is running at a controlled pace around the triangle.

- The drill continues until all the defensive backs have had a sufficient number of repetitions both left and right.

Coaching Points:

- Always check to see that the defensive backs are in their proper stances.

- Instruct the defensive backs to maintain the first tackle until they hear the coach's whistle.

- Make sure the defensive backs take the proper pursuit angle as they move to make the second tackle.

- The coach should move with the defenders and watch both of their tackles.
- Make sure the defensive backs practice proper fundamentals and techniques of safe tackling.

Safety Considerations:

- It is imperative that proper warm-up precede this drill.
- The drill area should be clear of all foreign articles.
- The drill should progress from half speed to full speed (not live).
- The coach should monitor closely the intensity of the drill.
- The coach should watch for and eliminate all unacceptable matchups as to size and athletic ability.
- Instruct all defensive backs as to proper fundamentals and techniques of safe tackling.

Variation:

- Can be used by all defensive positions.

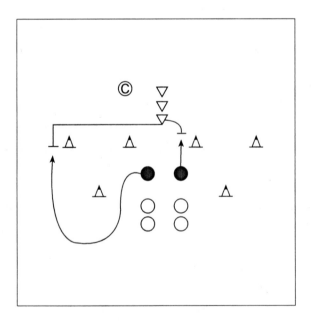

DRILL #59: TECHNIQUE-AND-AGILITY DRILL

Hugh "Duffy" Daugherty (Deceased)
Michigan State University
Overall Record: 109-69-5
National Champions: 1955, 1957, 1965, and 1966
National Coach of the Year: 1955 and 1965
College Football Hall of Fame: 1984
Amos Alonzo Stagg Award: 1985

Objective: To develop general agility, reaction, quickness, body control, and peripheral vision.

Equipment Needed: Four cones and a stopwatch

Description:

- Place four cones 20-yards apart to form a square.
- Position a row of defensive backs outside the cone at the right front of the square. (See diagram)
- The coach also stands at the front of the square.
- On the coach's command, the first defensive back assumes a good football position and then executes a *carioca* across the front of the drill area. He then runs backward to the second cone, *cariocas* to the third, and then sprints past the last cone. The defensive back is instructed to face the coach throughout the drill.
- The drill progresses from half speed to full speed.
- The drill continues until all the defensive backs have had a sufficient number of repetitions.

Coaching Points:

- Make sure the defensive backs execute the *cariocas* correctly.
- Insist that the defensive backs maintain the desired body position as they make their backward run.
- Make sure the defensive backs sprint past the last cone.
- Instruct the defensive backs always to face the front of the drill area throughout the drill.

Safety Considerations:

- Proper warm-up should precede the drill.
- Players with knee problems should be excused from this drill.
- Maintain a minimum distance of 15-yards between performing drill participants.

Variations:

- Can be used as a motivation drill by timing defensive backs once a week.
- Can be used as a general-agility drill.

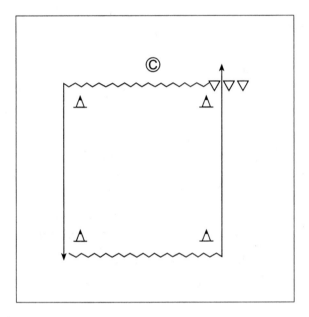

DRILL #60: STEM AND BREAK

Robert "Bobby" Wallace
University of North Alabama, Temple University
Overall Record: 94-68-1
National Champions: North Alabama 1993, 1994, and 1995
National Coach of the Year: North Alabama 1993, 1994, and 1995

Objective: To teach and practice the proper fundamentals and techniques of maintaining vertical and horizontal leverage on a receiver when in man-to-man coverage.

Equipment Needed: Four cones and a football

Description:

- Place four cones one-yard apart on a selected line of scrimmage.

- Align a defensive back five-yards behind and facing the cone on his far right. (See diagram)

- The coach holding a football is positioned on the opposite side of the cones and facing the defensive back. The coach remains stationary throughout the drill.

- Other defensive backs stand adjacent to the drill area.

- On the coach's cadence and snap count, the defensive back begins his backpedal.

- At a point during the backpedal determined by the coach, the coach moves the football laterally pointing in the direction of the second cone. The defensive back reacts to the coach's ball movements and *stems* back at 45-degree angle to the second cone.

- When the defensive back is positioned behind the second cone he once again goes into his backpedal and looks for and reacts to the coach's lateral-ball movement by *stemming* to the third cone.

- After the defensive back has *stemmed* from the backpedal in front of cone three, he plants his outside foot and breaks back upfield at a 45-degree angle catching the pass thrown by the coach.

- The drill continues until all the defensive backs have had a sufficient number of repetitions moving both to the left and the right.

Coaching Points:

- Always check to see that the defensive backs are in their proper stances.

- Instruct the defensive backs to execute the backpedal correctly by keeping their shoulders squared to the line of scrimmage.
- Instruct the defensive backs to execute the *stem* correctly by keeping their shoulders squared to the line of scrimmage as they gain width and depth while stepping laterally. (No crossover stepping is permitted.)
- Instruct the defensive backs to watch the coach and his ball movement at all times when moving to catch the thrown pass. Insist that the defensive backs drive off their back foot, catch the ball at its highest point, and yell oskie as they sprint for the touchdown.

Safety Considerations:

- Proper warm-up should precede the drill.
- The drill area should be clear of all foreign articles.

Variation:

- Can be used as a linebacker drill.

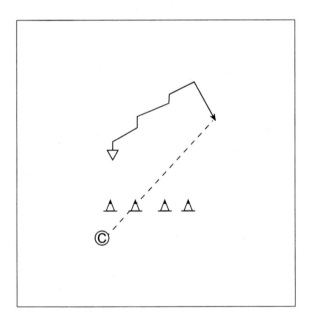

CHAPTER 9

Defensive End

Drills

DRILL #61: KEY DRILL

James C. "Jim" Young
University of Arizona, Purdue University, United States Military Academy
Overall Record: 120-71-2
National Coach of the Year: Army 1984
College Football Hall of Fame: 1999

Objective: To teach and practice the proper fundamentals and techniques of keying and reacting to the onside flow from the 50-defense.

Equipment Needed: Footballs

Description:

- Align a half-line offense (center, guard, tackle, tight end, and I backfield) over the football on a selected line of scrimmage.
- A defensive end takes his normal position over the tight end.
- Alternating defensive ends stand adjacent to the drill area.
- On the quarterback's cadence and ball snap, the offense executes one of five blocking schemes. The defensive end reads, reacts, and defeats the blocks of the different offensive players as shown in diagram. (A-tight end block, B-near back kick-out, C-offensive guard kick-out, D-running back kick-out, and E-tandem block.)
- The drill continues until all the drill participants have had a sufficient number of repetitions.
- The drill should be run with the offense in both left and right formations..

Coaching Points:

- Always check to see that the defensive ends are aligned correctly and are in their proper stances.
- Instruct the defensive ends as to their read progression (tight end, near back, guard, and tandem block).
- Insist that the defensive ends stay low and follow their keys in the proper sequence.

Safety Considerations:

- It is imperative that proper warm-up precede this drill.
- The drill area should be clear of all foreign articles.

- Full equipment should always be worn.
- The drill should progress from form to live blocking.
- The coach should monitor closely the intensity of the drill.
- Instruct the offensive players never to cut block the defensive ends.

Variations:

- Can be used as a form or live blocking drill.
- Can be used to key and react from the split end side.
- Can be used with various offensive sets.
- Can be used as an offensive drill.

A

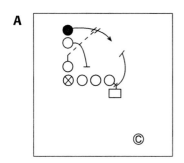

B

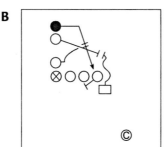

C

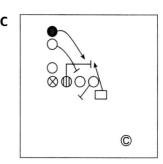

D

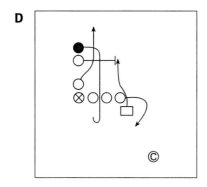

E

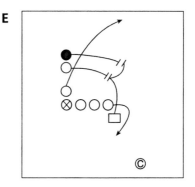

DRILL #62: SPEED RUSH AND FINISH

Chris Ault
University of Nevada
Overall Record: 163-63-1
National Coach of the Year: 1978 and 1991
College Football Hall of Fame: 2002

Objective: To teach and practice the proper fundamentals and techniques of rushing the passer from the tight end side.

Equipment Needed: Quarter-inch rubber hose and a football

Description:

- Align a center, a tackle, and a quarterback in their normal positions on a selected line of scrimmage.

- Place a quarter-inch rubber garden hose in a circle (approximately five yards in diameter) adjacent to the designated line of scrimmage so that the back of the circle is at a point four-yards behind the inside foot of the offensive tackle (see diagram).

- Align a defensive end at his normal position.

- Other drill participants stand adjacent to the drill area.

- On the quarterback's cadence and snap count, the offensive tackle executes his designated pass-protection block as the quarterback takes his five-step pass drop.

- The defensive end reacts to the snap count and drives past the block of the offensive tackle at the *intersect point* on the circle and strips the quarterback of the football (see diagram).

- The drill continues until all the defensive ends have had a sufficient number of repetitions from both left and right alignments.

Coaching Points:

- Always check to see that the defensive ends are aligned correctly and are in their proper stances.

- Instruct the defensive ends to lower their inside shoulder and to plant the outside foot as they accelerate through the block of the offensive tackle.

- Emphasize the importance of maintaining a tight corner at the *intersect point* of the circle.

- Instruct the quarterbacks to hold the football at different body alignments so that the defensive ends can practice stripping the football from various quarterback pass-throwing positions (above the shoulders and at the chest and waist areas).
- Insist that the defensive ends concentrate on the finish of the drill by first stripping the football from the quarterback and then recovering the football.

Safety Considerations:

- Proper warm-up should precede the drill.
- The drill should progress from formwork to full speed.
- Instruct the defensive ends not to hit or tackle the quarterback, but to only strip him of the football.
- When executing a live block with the tackle the rubber hose must be removed.

Variations:

- Can be used to read the draw and screen by inserting running backs and having the defensive end pursue the running back through the rush lanes for the draw and to the thrown football on screens.
- Can be used with the quarterback taking seven- and three-step pass drops by lengthening or shortening the diameter of the circle formed by the water hose.

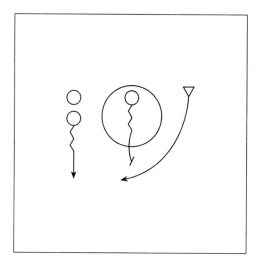

Robert "Bob" Reade
High School, Augustana College (IL)
Overall Record: 289-44-5
National Champions: 1983, 1984, 1985, and 1986
National Coach of the Year: 1983, 1984, 1985, and 1986
College Football Hall of Fame: 1998
Amos Alonzo Stagg Award: 1998

Objective: To teach and practice the proper fundamentals and techniques of defending the split-back veer-offensive set.

Equipment Needed: Hand shield and line marker

Description:

- Position a quarterback, center, tight end, and two running backs in their normal split-back veer alignment on a selected line of scrimmage.

- A line marker is placed just behind the hip of the offensive tackle position (mesh point).

- Position a defensive end, holding a hand shield, in his normal alignment over the outside hip of the tight end. (The hand shield will allow the defensive end to attack the mesh point and the quarterback at full speed and in a safe manner.) (See diagram.)

- Other drill participants stand adjacent to the drill area.

- The coach is positioned opposite the offense and two-yards behind the mesh point.

- On the quarterback's cadence and snap count, the offense runs the designated split-back veer play.

- The defensive end reacts to the snap count and drives through the *V* of the neck and shoulder areas of the tight end and directly to the mesh point.

- If the tight end reads inside veer, he continues straight down the line and attacks the quarterback.

- If the quarterback fakes the outside veer and drops back to pass, the defensive end redirects his charge upfield and pressures the quarterback.

- If the quarterback's action is away, the defensive end attacks him while looking for the bootleg.

- The drill continues until all the defensive ends have had a sufficient number of repetitions from both the left and right alignments.

Coaching Points:

- Always check to see that the defensive ends are aligned correctly and are in their proper stances.
- Instruct the defensive ends to first focus on the inside-veer mesh point and then the quarterback.
- Insist that the defensive ends drive through the *V* of the tight end and not to step around him.

Safety Considerations:

- Proper warm-up should precede the drill.
- The drill area should be clear of all foreign articles.
- The drill should progress from formwork to live work.

Variation:

- Can be used to pressure a variety of offensive schemes.

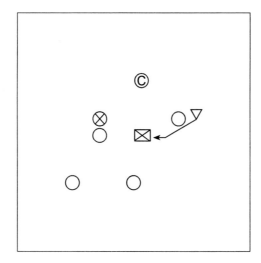

DRILL #64: KEYING AND REACTING

Ronald "Skip" Schipper
High School, Central College (IA)
Overall Record: 320-78-5
National Champions: 1974
College Football Hall of Fame: 2000
AFCA President: 1994

Objective: To teach and practice the proper fundamentals and techniques of keying and reacting to various blocking schemes from the 50-defense.

Equipment Needed: Football

Description:

- Align a half-line offense (center, guard, tackle, tight end, and a designated backfield) in their normal positions on a selected line of scrimmage.
- Align a defensive end in his normal position over the tight end.
- Other defensive ends stand adjacent to the drill area or may serve as offensive personnel.
- On the quarterback's cadence and snap count, the offense executes one of six blocking schemes. (A-drive block, B-cross block, C-guard kick-out, D-back kick-out, E-sweep block, and F-pass block. See diagram.)
- The drill continues until all the defensive ends have had a sufficient number of repetitions reading all blocking schemes from both left and right formations.

Coaching Points:

- Always check to see that the defensive ends are aligned correctly and are in their proper stances.
- Make sure the defensive ends follow their correct read progressions (the tight end, tackle, guard, and near back).
- Instruct the defensive ends to react quickly on the ball snap, to always stay low, and to read and deliver a forearm blow on the approaching blocker.

Safety Considerations:

- Proper warm-up should precede the drill.
- Full equipment should be worn and chinstraps snapped.
- The drill area should be clear of all foreign articles.

- The drill should progress from form blocking to live blocking.
- The coach should monitor closely the intensity of the drill.

Variations:

- Can be used against various backfield sets.
- Can be used as an offensive drill.
- Can be used as a weakside defensive end drill.

A

B

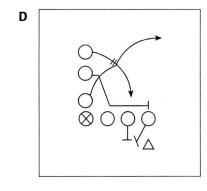

C

D

E

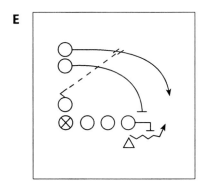

F

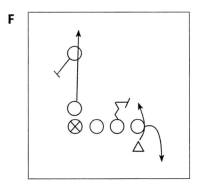

CHAPTER 10

Linebacker

Drills

DRILL #65: BREAK ON BALL

Patrick Fain "Pat" Dye
East Carolina University, University of Wyoming, Auburn University
Overall Record: 153-62-5
National Coach of the Year: Auburn, 1983

Objective: To teach and practice the proper fundamentals and techniques of taking the proper pass drop, reading the quarterback, breaking on the football, and intercepting the pass.

Equipment Needed: Three footballs

Description:

- Align a quarterback (coach) holding a football at the midpoint of a selected line of scrimmage.
- Position a row of receivers one-yard outside the hash mark and perpendicular to the line of scrimmage.
- A linebacker is placed in his normal alignment to the receiver side of the field (see diagram).
- Other linebackers stand adjacent to their drill area.
- On the cadence and snap count, the quarterback (coach) executes an eight-yard pass drop and passes the football to the wide receiver that is running either a 12-yard curl or a crossing route.
- The linebacker reacts to the snap count, executes his pass drop, reads the quarterback, and breaks on the football for the interception.
- The drill continues until all the linebackers have had a sufficient number of repetitions.
- The drill should be conducted both left and right.

Coaching Points:

- Always check to see that the linebackers are aligned correctly and are in their proper stances.
- Instruct the linebackers to set up simultaneously with the quarterback.
- Insist that the linebackers take the correct angle when breaking on the football.
- The passer should exaggerate his shoulder turn so linebackers will get a good read.

Safety Considerations:

- Proper warm-up should precede the drill.
- The drill area should be clear of all foreign articles.
- Instruct the linebackers to break in front of the receiver and to avoid all collisions.

Variations:

- Can be used with wide receiver running only the ending step of the patterns.
- Can be used as a wide receiver drill.

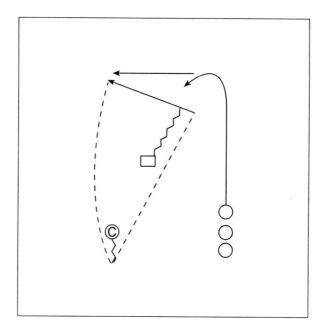

DRILL #66: LINEBACKER TOSS-SWEEP PURSUIT

Richard "Dick" MacPherson
University of Massachusetts, Syracuse University, New England Patriots
Overall Record: 110-94-5
National Coach of the Year: Syracuse 1987

Objective: To teach and practice the proper fundamentals and techniques of filling the gap and pursuing on the toss sweep.

Equipment Needed: Two large blocking dummies and footballs

Description:

- Align offensive personnel (quarterback, center, two guards, tight end, fullback, and tailback) over the football on a selected line of scrimmage.
- Lay two dummies at the offensive tackle positions.
- Place linebackers and defensive ends in their normal alignments over the offense. (To emphasize inside linebacker play, have defensive ends hold hand shields.)
- Other drill participants stand adjacent to the drill area.
- On the quarterback's cadence and ball snap, the offense executes the toss sweep as the defensive personnel read, react, defeat blockers, and pursue the ballcarrier. (See diagram)
- The drill continues until all the drill participants have had a sufficient number of repetitions.
- The sweep should be executed to both the strongside and the weakside of the formation and from both left and right alignment.

Coaching Points:

- Always check to see that all personnel are aligned correctly and are in their proper stances. (Encourage linebackers and defensive ends to show blitz.)
- Instruct the playside linebackers to mirror the play, defeat the block of the onside guard, and pursue the ballcarrier.
- The backside linebackers are instructed to seal the playside A gap, defeat the cut block of the guard, and pursue the ballcarrier. (Caution backside linebackers not to get caught up in the line.)
- Insist that the linebackers maintain a good football position as they react and pursue each play.
- Make sure that all the linebackers react and pursue correctly on all plays.

Safety Considerations:

- It is imperative that proper warm-up precede this drill.
- The drill area should be clear of all foreign articles.
- The drill should progress from form blocking to live blocking.
- The coach should monitor closely the intensity of the drill.
- Instruct the linebackers as to the proper fundamentals and techniques in defeating blockers and executing safe tackles.
- Instruct the linebackers only to *thud up* on the ballcarriers.
- A quick whistle is imperative with this drill.

Variations:

- Can be used against the power sweep and other selected plays.
- Can be used as a defensive end drill.
- Can be used as an offensive guard drill.
- Can be used as a combination and team-play drill.

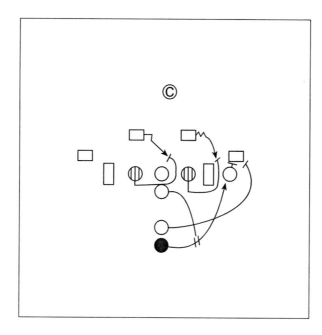

DRILL #67: PURSUIT DRILL

Dennis E. Green
Northwestern University, Stanford University, Minnesota Vikings
Overall Record: 123-125-0
National Football League Coach of the Year: 1992 and 1998

Objective: To teach and practice the proper fundamentals and techniques of pursuing to the football, defeating a blocker, and executing a tackle.

Equipment Needed: Six large blocking dummies, two hand shields, and a line-spacing strip

Description:

- Position two linebackers in their regular alignments across from a selected line of scrimmage.
- Other linebackers stand adjacent to the drill area.
- Lay two large blocking dummies in the path of each linebacker's pursuit route (two-yards separate the blocking dummies). Two players, holding hand shields, stand adjacent to the dummy area. Stand another held dummy 10-yards behind each shield holder. (See diagram)
- On the coach's command, the two linebackers pursue over and through the dummies, defeat the players with the hand shield, and sprint to and tackle the stand up dummy.
- The drill continues until all the linebackers have had a sufficient number of repetitions.
- The drill should be conducted both left and right.

Coaching Points:

- Always check to see that the linebackers are aligned correctly and are in their proper stances.
- Make sure the linebackers maintain a squared-shoulder relationship to the line of scrimmage as they pursue over and through the dummy area.
- Instruct the linebackers to fight through the hand shields and not to run around them.
- Insist that the drill be conducted at full speed.

Safety Considerations:

- Proper warm-up should precede the drill.

- The drill area should be clear of all foreign articles.

- Instruct all the linebackers as to the proper fundamentals and techniques of safe tackling.

- Instruct the dummy holders to release the dummies as the tackles are being executed.

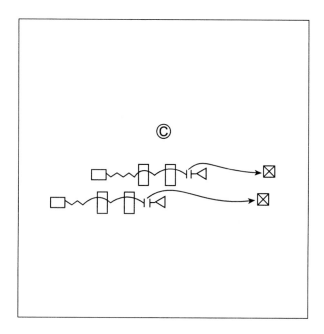

DRILL #68: SHED TACKLE

Bill G. Mallory
Miami University (OH), University of Colorado,
Northern Illinois University, Indiana University
Overall Record: 168-129-4

Objective: To teach and practice the proper fundamentals and techniques of defeating a blocker, pursuing the ballcarrier, and executing a tackle.

Equipment Needed: Four cones and footballs

Description:

- Place two cones 10-yards apart on a selected line of scrimmage. Another cone is placed three-yards outside the first two cones (see diagram).
- Position a blocker midway between the two inside cones. A ballcarrier, holding a football, stands eight-yards behind the blocker.
- A linebacker is positioned four yards in front of the blocker.
- Other linebackers stand adjacent to the drill area.
- The coach stands behind the linebackers and signals the offensive players as to the snap count and direction of the play.
- On the coach's cadence and snap count, the blocker drives out of his stance and executes a drive block on the linebacker. The ballcarrier runs between the two cones as designated by the coach.
- The linebacker reacts to and sheds the blocker and then pursues and tackles the ballcarrier.
- The drill continues until all the linebackers have had a sufficient number of repetitions.

Coaching Points:

- Always check to see that the linebackers are aligned correctly and are in their proper stances.
- Instruct the linebackers to shed all blocks to the inside.
- Make sure the linebackers maintain a squared-shoulder relationship to the line of scrimmage throughout the drill.
- Make sure the linebackers practice proper fundamentals and techniques of block shedding and safe tackling.

Safety Considerations:

- It is imperative that proper warm-up precede this drill.
- The drill area should be clear of all foreign articles.
- The drill should progress from formwork to live work.
- The coach should watch for and eliminate all unacceptable matchups as to size and athletic ability.
- The coach should monitor closely the intensity of the drill.
- Instruct all the linebackers as to the proper fundamentals and techniques of block shedding and safe tackling.
- A quick whistle is imperative with this drill.
- The training staff should be placed on alert.

Variations:

- Can be used as a form or live blocking and tackling drill.
- Can be used as a goal line drill.
- Can be used without blockers having linebackers pursue over and through dummies and execute the tackle.
- Can be used as an offensive line drill.

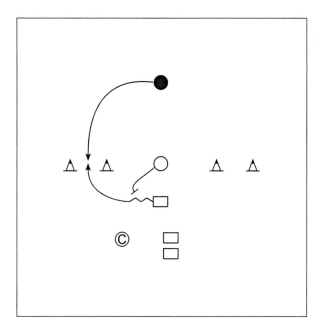

DRILL #69: SPOT-LATERAL WAVE DRILL

Jimmy Johnson
Oklahoma State University, University of Miami, Dallas Cowboys, Miami Dolphins
Overall Record: 171-102-2
National Champions: Miami 1987
Super Bowl XXVII, XXVIII Champions
National Football League Coach of the Year: Dallas 1990, 1991, and 1992

Objective: To teach and practice the proper fundamentals and techniques in executing the correct pass drop and breaking on and intercepting a pass.

Equipment Needed: Footballs

Description:

- Align a defensive linebacker in his stance across from a selected line of scrimmage.
- A quarterback (coach), holding a football, stands five yards in front of linebacker. He instructs linebacker to execute a pass drop to either the hook or curl zone.
- Other linebackers form a line to the right of the coach (see diagram).
- On the quarterback's (coach's) pass drop, the linebacker moves to the designated pass coverage zone, works his feet in place, and watches the quarterback. As the quarterback looks and turns his shoulders, both left and right, the linebacker reacts and moves in the corresponding direction.
- The quarterback looks and turns his shoulders a final time and passes the football.
- The linebacker reads, reacts, and breaks on the football, intercepting the pass at its highest point.
- The drill continues until all the linebackers have had a sufficient number of repetitions.
- The drill should be conducted both left and right and from various field positions.

Coaching Points:

- Always check to see that the linebackers are in their proper stances.
- Instruct the linebackers always to open with the outside foot, to watch the quarterback, and to sprint to their designated pass coverage zone.
- Insist that the linebackers maintain a squared-shoulder relationship to the line of scrimmage when they complete their pass drop.

- Instruct the linebackers to yell *pass* when they read the play, *ball* when the football is thrown, and *oskie* when they make the interception.
- Insist that the linebackers intercept the football at its highest point and sprint past the line of scrimmage after the interception is made.

Safety Considerations:

- Proper warm-up should precede the drill.
- The drill area should be clear of all foreign articles.
- Helmets should be worn with chinstraps snapped.

Variations:

- Can be used with various quarterback pass drops and linebacker coverages.
- Can be used as a defensive back drill.

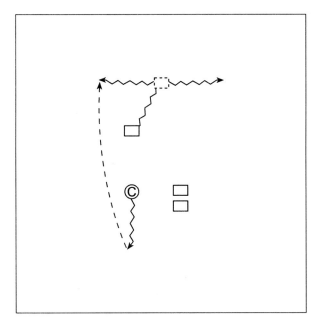

DRILL #70: TRIANGLE DRILL

Darrell K. Royal
Edmonton Eskimos, Mississippi State University,
University of Washington, University of Texas
Overall Record: 196-64-5
National Champions: Texas 1963, 1969, and 1970
National Coach of the Year: Texas 1961, 1963, and 1970
College Football Hall Of Fame: 1983
AFCA President: 1975

Objective: To teach and practice the proper fundamentals and techniques of gaining separation from a blocker in executing a forearm-shoulder blow.

Equipment Needed: One large blocking dummy

Description:

- Align three linebackers in a football position in a triangle as shown in the diagram. One yard separates each of the linebackers.
- Lay a blocking dummy on the ground behind the linebacker designated as the defender. The two linebackers forming the base of the triangle are designated blockers.
- Other linebackers stand adjacent to the drill area.
- The coach is positioned behind the defender and signals the blockers either to come one at a time or in a predetermined sequence to block the linebacker.
- The defender reacts to and defeats each block with a forearm-shoulder blow.
- After the defender has executed a desired number of forearm-shoulder blows, the three drill participants rotate clockwise with another linebacker becoming the defender.
- The drill continues until all the linebackers have had a sufficient number of repetitions.
- The drill should progress from walk-through to half speed to full speed.

Coaching Points:

- Always check to see that the linebackers are in a good football position.
- Make sure that the defenders keep their shoulders low and squared to the blockers throughout the drill.

- Instruct the linebackers to take short jab steps as they move to defeat the blockers. After contact is made, the other foot should be brought forward.
- Instruct the defender to use their hands in gaining separation from the blocker.

Safety Considerations:

- It is imperative that proper warm-up precede this drill.
- The drill should progress from formwork to live work.
- The coach should monitor closely the intensity of the drill.
- The coach should look for and eliminate all unacceptable matchups as to size and athletic ability.
- Instruct all the linebackers as to the proper fundamentals and techniques of delivering a forearm-shoulder blow.

Variations:

- Can incorporate a tackling drill on a ballcarrier after gaining separation from the final blocker.
- Can be used as a defensive line and end drill.

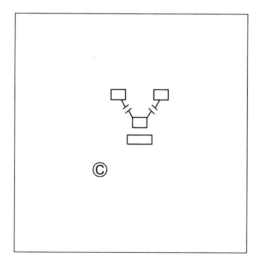

CHAPTER 11

Defensive Line

Drills

DRILL #71: CONTAIN DRILL

Bill McCartney
University of Colorado
Overall Record: 93-55-5
National Champions: 1990
National Coach of the Year: 1989

Objective: To teach and practice interior pursuit with special emphasis on reacting to the ball snap and taking the proper angle to the ballcarrier.

Equipment Needed: 20 cones and four footballs

Description:

- Align ten cones, one each, on every five-yard line downfield from a selected line of scrimmage. All cones are placed five yards from each sideline (see diagram).

- A center and a quarterback are positioned over a football at midfield.

- A runner, holding a football, is positioned between cones and sidelines. A manager, or another player, is placed behind each runner.

- Align the defensive front in a huddle behind the line of scrimmage.

- Alternating defensive fronts stand adjacent to the drill area.

- On the coach's command, the defensive front breaks the huddle with an assigned defensive call and takes their positions over the football.

- On the cadence and ball snap, the quarterback takes a five-yard pass drop and passes the football to the manager on either sideline. When the manager catches the football, the ballcarrier on that sideline sprints downfield.

- The defensive linemen react to the ball snap and carry out the initial steps of the designated defense called in the huddle. They then take their proper pursuit angle to the ballcarrier.

- When the pursuers get to the ballcarrier, they break down and wait for the coach's whistle to end the drill.

- The drill continues with alternating defensive fronts pursuing both left and right from midfield and both hash marks.

Coaching Points:

- Always check to see that all personnel are aligned correctly and are in their proper stances.

- The drill should progress from walk-through to full speed.
- Make sure the defenders execute the initial steps of the assigned defense before going in pursuit.

Safety Considerations:

- Proper warm-up should precede the drill.
- The drill area should be clear of all foreign articles. This includes the sideline areas.

Variations:

- Can be used by the entire defensive team.
- Can align ballcarriers at various positions on the sideline or at other positions on the field.

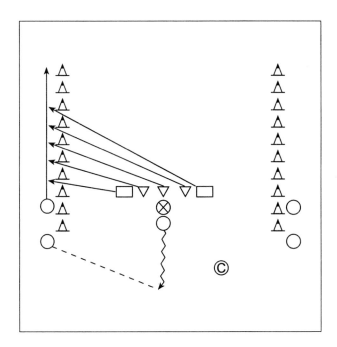

DRILL #72: DEFEATING THE BLOCK

William D. "Bill" Murray (Deceased)
[Drill submitted by Dr. Michael "Mike" McGee]
High School, University of Delaware, Duke University
Overall Record: 213-77-14
College Football Hall of Fame: 1974
Amos Alonzo Stagg Award: 1971
AFCA President: 1963
AFCA Executive Director: 1966-1981

Objective: To teach and practice proper fundamentals and techniques of defeating the drive block. The drill stresses the importance of achieving a shoe-to-shoe relationship to the opponent before defeating his block. It also stresses the necessity of maintaining a parallel (squared) shoulder and hip relationship to the line of scrimmage until the direction of the ballcarrier is determined. The drill is conducted in two stages.

Equipment Needed: Footballs

Description:

Stage I–Ballcarrier's Path is Determined

- Align a blocker and ballcarrier in their proper relationship to a selected line of scrimmage.
- A defensive lineman is placed in one of three positions: behind the blocker, head-up the blocker, and ahead of the blocker (see diagrams A, B, and C).
- On the coach's cadence, the defender reacts to and defeats the block of the offensive lineman and then executes the tackle on the ballcarrier.
- The drill continues until all the drill participants have had a sufficient number of repetitions.
- The drill should be executed both left and right.

Stage II–Ballcarrier's Path is Undetermined

- All personnel are aligned in the same relative position as in Stage I, procedures 1 and 2.
- In Stage II, however, the path of the runner is undetermined and the runner can cut off the offensive lineman's block either left or right (see diagrams D, E, and F).
- On the coach's cadence, the defensive lineman reacts to and defeats the block of the offensive lineman and executes the tackle on the ballcarrier.
- The drill continues until all the linemen have had a sufficient number of repetitions.

- The drill should be run both left and right.

Coaching Points:

- Always check to see that the defensive linemen are aligned correctly and are in their proper stances.
- It is imperative that the defenders achieve a shoe-to-shoe relationship with the blocker before extension.
- The defenders should use only the amount of force necessary to defeat the blocks and then gain separation for the tackle.
- Instruct the defensive linemen to maintain a squared-shoulder and hip relationship to the ballcarrier until the ballcarrier's running path has been determined.
- Make sure the defenders use the proper fundamentals and techniques in executing the tackle.

Safety Considerations:

- It is imperative that proper warm-up precede this drill.
- Instruct all the defenders as to the proper fundamentals and techniques of defeating a block and executing a safe tackle.
- The drill should progress from formwork to live work.
- The coach should watch for and eliminate all unacceptable matchups as to size and athletic ability.
- The coach should monitor closely the intensity of the drill.

Variations:

- Can be used as a form or live drill.
- Can be used as an offensive line drill.

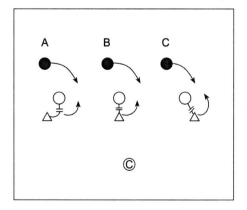
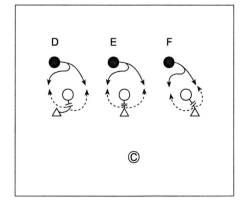

DRILL #73: TWO-MAN SLED HIT PROGRESSION

Leonard J. "Len" Casanova (Deceased)
Santa Clara University, University of Pittsburgh, University of Oregon
Overall Record: 104-97-10
College Football Hall of Fame: 1977
Amos Alonzo Stagg Award: 1990
AFCA President: 1964

Objective: To teach and practice the proper fundamentals and techniques in the execution of the forearm-shoulder blow.

Equipment Needed: Two-man sled

Description:

- Position two rows of defensive linemen behind the pads of a two-man sled. The drill is conducted in six phases as follows:
  - *Forearm Lift.* The first two linemen assume the football position in front of the pads of the sled and on the coach's command, strike the pad using only the inside fist and forearm.
  - *Hip Thrust.* The paired drill participants assume knee stances sitting back on their heels. On the coach's command, they lean forward at a 45-degree angle and strike a forearm blow to the pads. In the execution of the blow, the head is up, the outside arm is thrown forward, and the hips are extended thrusting the belt buckle toward the pad.
  - *Step and Hit.* In this phase, the defensive linemen assume their normal stances and on the coach's command, step with the inside foot as they strike the pad with a forearm blow. The outside foot does not move.
  - *Hit and Gather.* Repeat procedures in the preceding phase bringing the outside foot to a good football position on the sled. Hold for four seconds.
  - *Hit, Gather, and Move Feet.* Repeat the preceding two phases working both feet in place without moving the sled.
  - *Drive.* Repeat the preceding three phases with linemen driving the sled until the coach blows his whistle. The drill participants now execute a seat roll to complete drill.
- The drill continues until all the defensive linemen have had a sufficient number of repetitions of all six drill phases.
- The drill should be conducted with the linemen executing both left and right forearm-shoulder blows.

Coaching Points:

- Always check to see that the linemen are in their proper stances in the last four phases (*Step and Hit* through *Drive*).
- Instruct the linemen to keep their shoulders square to the pad of the sled throughout all phases of the drill.
- In contacting the pad, make sure the arm is bent to form a 90-degree blocking-angle surface with the wrist rotated inward.
- Insist that the linemen maintain a good hitting position with the head up and feet apart throughout this drill.
- The coach should always view the drill from behind the drill participants.

Safety Considerations:

- Proper warm-up should precede the drill.
- Helmets should be worn with chinstraps snapped.
- Instruct all the linemen as to the proper fundamentals and techniques of blocking a sled.
- The sled should be checked periodically for possible maintenance and repairs.

Variation:

- Can be used as a defensive end and linebacker drill.

DRILL #74: HEADS

Mike Kelly
University of Dayton
Overall Record: 195-40-1
National Champions: 1989
National Coach of the Year: 1989 and 1991

Objective: To teach and practice the proper fundamentals and techniques of reading and reacting to various blocking schemes presented to a noseguard by a center and two guards.

Equipment Needed: Flash cards

Description:

- Align a center and two offensive guards in their normal alignment on a selected line of scrimmage.
- A noseguard is aligned in his normal position over the center.
- Other noseguards stand adjacent to the drill area or may be used as offensive personnel.
- A coach stands behind the noseguard holding various center-guard blocking scheme flash cards.
- On the coach's cadence and snap count, the center and guards execute the designated center-guard blocking scheme that was shown on the flash card.
- The noseguard reads and reacts to the various blocking schemes executed by the center and guards.
- The drill continues until all the noseguards have had a sufficient number of repetitions.

Coaching Points:

- Always check to see that the noseguards are aligned correctly and are in their proper stances.
- In the teaching phase of the drill, the coach may alert the noseguards as to which blocking scheme the center and guard will execute.
- Instruct the noseguards to always keep their shoulders squared to the line of scrimmage as they read and react to the different blocking schemes.

Safety Considerations:

- Proper warm-up should precede the drill.
- Helmets should be worn and chinstraps snapped.
- The coach should place emphasis on the fact that this is a read-and-reaction drill and not a contact drill.

Variation:

- Can be used as an offensive center and guard-blocking drill.

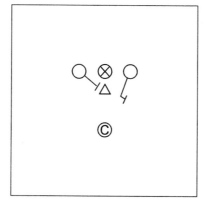

CHAPTER 12

Tackling

Drills

DRILL #75: FACE DRILL

Ara Raoul Parseghian
Miami University (OH), Northwestern University, University of Notre Dame
Overall Record: 170-58-6
National Champions: Notre Dame 1964, 1966, and 1973
National Coach of the Year: Notre Dame 1964
College Football Hall of Fame: 1980
Amos Alonzo Stagg Award: 1997

Objective: To teach and practice the proper fundamentals and techniques of open-field tackling. Incorporated are skills related to running, agility, reaction, and quickness.

Equipment Needed: Three large blocking dummies

Description:

- Position three held dummies five-yards apart on a selected line of scrimmage. The coach holds the middle dummy.
- Align a row of tacklers 20 yards downfield, facing the middle dummy.
- On the coach's command, the first tackler sprints straight for the middle dummy.
- As he approaches the dummy area, the coach signals the tackler to move either left or right by tilting his dummy.
- The tackler reacts and executes the tackle on the dummy to the designated side.
- The drill continues until all the drill participants have had a sufficient number of tackles.

Coaching Points:

- Make sure that all the drill participants square up to the dummy before executing the tackle.
- Emphasize the importance of wrapping the arms on all tackles.
- Make sure that all personnel practice the proper fundamentals and techniques of safe tackling.
- Insist that the drill be conducted at full speed.

Safety Considerations:

- Proper warm-up should precede the drill.
- The drill area should be clear of all foreign articles.

- Instruct all the personnel as to the proper fundamentals and techniques of safe tackling.
- Dummy holders should be instructed to release dummies as each tackle is being executed.

Variations:

- Can vary the distance at which tacklers line up from dummy area.
- Can vary the distance between dummies.
- Coach can signal tacklers at various times, or can even delay signal and instruct tacklers to break down working their feet, before tilting the dummy.

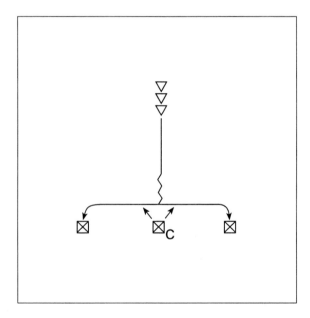

DRILL #76: SHUFFLE TACKLE

Barry Alvarez
University of Wisconsin
Overall Record: 84-55-4
National Coach of the Year: 1993

Objective: To teach and practice the proper fundamentals and techniques of tackling. Incorporated are skills related to shuffling the feet, keeping the shoulders squared, keeping an inside-out leverage on the ballcarrier, and taking the correct angle to the ballcarrier when making a tackle.

Equipment Needed: Five large block dummies and hand shields

Description:

- Lay five block dummies two to two-and-a-half-yards apart and perpendicular to a selected line of scrimmage.
- Position a row of tacklers to the left of and one-and-a-half-yards behind and facing the row of dummies. Ballcarriers are aligned in a row, holding hand shields, in a similar position on the opposite side of the row of dummies (see diagram).
- On the coach's command, the first ballcarrier runs to the end of the row of dummies and back to the starting point.
- The tackler, shuffling his feet, mirrors the run of the ballcarrier to the end of the row of dummies and back.
- The ballcarrier now runs to and through any pair of the dummies as the tackler *buzzes* his feet and moves to tackle the ballcarrier.
- The drill continues until all the tacklers have had a sufficient number of repetitions from both left and right.

Coaching Points:

- Instruct the tacklers to maintain a good football position throughout the drill.
- After the tacklers have mirrored the ballcarrier back to the starting point, instruct the tacklers to *buzz* their feet and to be patient as they wait to see which pair of dummies the ballcarrier runs between.
- Instruct the tacklers to maintain a position on the backside hip of the ballcarrier and always approach him from an inside-out position, thus taking away the cutback angle.
- Make sure all the tacklers practice the proper fundamentals and techniques of safe tackling.

Safety Considerations:

- It is imperative that proper warm-up precedes this drill.
- Instruct all personnel as to the proper fundamentals and technique of safe tackling.
- The drill should progress from form tackling to live tackling.
- The coach should monitor closely the intensity of the drill.
- The coach should watch for and eliminate all unacceptable matchups as to size and athletic ability.

Variation:

- Can be used with ballcarriers holding hand shields for protection.

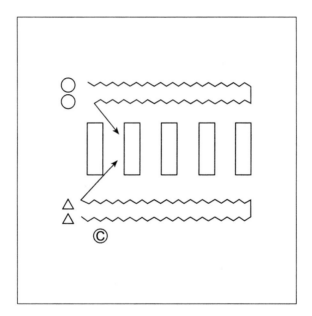

DRILL #77: TACKLING DRILL

Eddie Robinson
Grambling State University
Overall Record: 408-165-15
National Black College Champions: 1955, 1967, 1972, 1974,
1975, 1977, 1980, 1983, and 1992
National Coach of the Year: 1992
National Black College Coach of the Year: 1967, 1972, 1974,
1975, 1977, 1980, 1983, and 1995
College Football Hall of Fame: 1997
Amos Alonzo Stagg Award: 1982
Tuss McLaughry Award: 1996
AFCA President: 1976

Objective: To teach and practice the proper fundamentals and techniques of tackling. Incorporated are skills related to reaction, agility, and quickness.

Equipment Needed: Five large blocking dummies and footballs

Description:

- Lay five blocking dummies three-feet apart on a selected line of scrimmage (see diagram).
- Position a line of tacklers adjacent to the row of dummies and a row of ballcarriers seven yards in front of and facing the tacklers.
- The coach, holding a football, stands four yards in front of the ballcarriers.
- On the coach's command, the first tackler positions himself flat on his back with his head toward the first ballcarrier.
- On the cadence and snap count, the coach pitches the football to the first ballcarrier, who runs to the end of the dummy area and cuts upfield.
- The tackler reacts to the coach's cadence, springs to his feet, shuffles over and through the dummies and executes a tackle on the running back.
- The drill continues until all the tacklers have had a sufficient number of repetitions, shuffling over and through the dummies from both left and right alignment.

Coaching Points:

- Make sure the tacklers maintain a good football position as they shuffle over and through the dummies. Crossover stepping should be discouraged.
- Make sure the tacklers practice proper fundamentals and techniques of safe tackling.

- The tackle should be viewed from various angles.
- Insist that tacklers shuffle through the dummies at full speed.

Safety Considerations:

- It is imperative that proper warm-up precede this drill.
- The drill should progress from form tackling to live tackling.
- The coach should monitor closely the intensity of the drill.
- The coach should watch for and eliminate all unacceptable matchups as to size and athletic ability.
- Instruct all tacklers as to proper fundamentals and techniques of safe tackling.
- The training staff should be placed on special alert.

Variations:

- Can be used as a form or live tackling drill.
- Can be used with a lead blocker and ballcarrier.
- Can be used with a player holding a hand dummy and jamming the tackler as he gets off the ground.

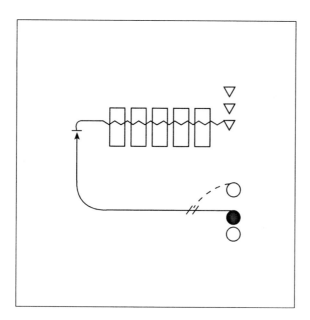

PART III
GENERAL DRILLS

CHAPTER 13

Combination and

Team-Play Drills

DRILL #78: EIGHT-ON-EIGHT DRILL

Frank J. Howard (Deceased)
Clemson University
Overall Record: 165-118-12
College Football Hall of Fame: 1989

Objective: To teach and practice various running and passing plays utilizing selected offensive and defensive personnel.

Equipment Needed: Football

Description:

- Align offensive personnel (center, tackles, tight end, running backs, flanker, split end, and quarterback) over the football at the midpoint of a selected line of scrimmage (see diagram). It should be noted that the center is used only to snap the football.
- Position a defensive team (tackles, ends, and a four-deep secondary) over the offense.
- Other drill participants stand adjacent to the drill area.
- On the quarterback's cadence and ball snap, the offense executes selected plays called in the huddle.
- The defense reacts to and tries to stop the offense.
- The drill continues with the offense executing selected running and passing plays from various alignments and from different positions on the field.

Coaching Points:

- Always check to see that all the drill participants are aligned correctly and are in their proper stances.
- Make sure all play assignments are carried out correctly.

Safety Considerations:

- It is imperative that proper warm-up precede this drill.
- The drill area should be clear of all foreign articles.
- The coach should look for and eliminate all unacceptable matchups as to size and athletic ability.
- Insist that all blocks be executed above the waist.

- The coach should monitor closely the intensity of the drill.
- A quick whistle is imperative with this drill.
- The training staff should be placed on special alert.

Variations:

- Can be used with defenders holding dummies.
- Can be used as a defensive drill.

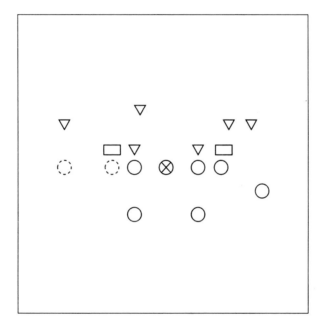

DRILL #79: HALF-LINE OFFENSE AND DEFENSE

Earle D. Bruce
The University of Tampa, Iowa State University, The Ohio State University,
University of Northern Iowa, Colorado State University
Overall Record: 154-90-2
National Coach of the Year: Ohio State 1979
College Football Hall of Fame: 2002

Objective: To teach and practice the proper fundamentals and techniques of offensive and defensive football as they relate to a half-line scrimmage situation.

Equipment Needed: Footballs

Description:

- Align two half-line offenses (tight end side and split end side) over a football on selected lines of scrimmage (see diagrams).
- Position a defense over each offense.
- Alternating units are positioned on the sideline.
- The competitive units (first offense versus second defense or first offense versus first defense, etc.) must be determined.
- Coaches stand adjacent to their various areas of responsibility.
- Offensive and defensive units huddle before each down to select plays and defensive assignments.
- The drill should be run under complete game conditions using down-and-distance situations.
- The drill should be conducted from both left and right formations and from different field positions.
- The drill continues until all half-line units have executed a sufficient number of plays.

Coaching Points:

- Always check to see that all the personnel are aligned correctly and are in their proper stances.
- Instruct the signal callers to use only basic offensive plays and defensive alignments.
- Make sure all the appropriate personnel use the proper fundamentals and techniques of running, blocking, block shedding, and tackling.

- Intensity and toughness should be encouraged with each play.
- If offense does not make a first down in four plays, all personnel should rotate.

Safety Considerations:

- It is imperative that proper warm-up precede this drill.
- The drill areas should be clear of all foreign articles. This includes the sideline areas.
- The coach should watch for and eliminate all unacceptable matchups as to size and athletic ability.
- Insist that all blocks be executed above the waist.
- Tackling is permitted only on the line of scrimmage.
- The coach should monitor closely the intensity of the drill.
- A quick whistle is imperative with this drill.
- The training staff should be placed on special alert.

Variations:

- Can emphasize the offense by having defenders hold dummies.
- Can vary defensive alignments and coverages.
- Can be used to accent various down-and-distance situations such as goal line, short yardage, and third-and-long.

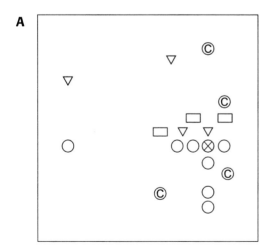
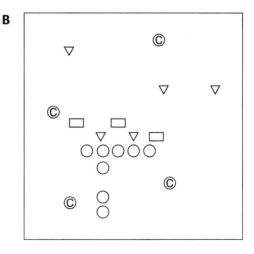

DRILL #80: THREE-ON-THREE DRILL

Jerry David Claiborne (Deceased)
Virginia Polytechnic Institute, University of Maryland, University of Kentucky
Overall Record: 179-122-8
College Football Hall of Fame: 1999
AFCA President: 1980

Objective: To teach and practice the proper fundamentals and techniques of the inside running game as they relate to both offense and defense. Incorporated are skills related to drive and cutoff blocks for offensive linemen and tight ends, reading blocks and running to daylight for running backs, handoffs for quarterbacks, and defeating a blocker, pursuit, and tackling for defensive personnel.

Equipment Needed: Footballs

Description:

- Mark off a drill area 10-yards square.

- Align an offense (three blockers, a quarterback, and two running backs) at the midpoint of the designated starting point of the drill area. If a center is among the three blockers, he lines up in the middle and over a football. If there is not a center, the quarterback holds the football at the center-quarterback exchange position (see diagram).

- Position three defensive players (linemen, defensive ends, or linebackers) nose-on-nose across from the three offensive blockers.

- Other drill participants stand adjacent to the drill area and yell encouragement to their teammates.

- A coach stands behind the defense and signals to the offense the snap count and the dive play to run.

- Other position coaches are aligned in adjacent areas.

- On the quarterback's cadence and snap count, the offense executes the designated dive play. The defensive personnel react, pursue, and tackle the ballcarrier.

- The offense is given three downs in which to cover the 10 yards for the score. When each down is completed, the football is placed at the point where the ballcarrier was tackled and midway between the two side boundaries. After a score or three downs, the coach can change personnel at his discretion.

- The drill continues until all the drill participants have had a sufficient number of repetitions.

Coaching Points:

- Always check to see that all the personnel are aligned correctly and are in their proper stances.
- Playside blockers are instructed to use a drive block and other blockers to use cutoff blocks.
- Ballcarriers should read blockers and run for daylight.
- Insist that all defenders drive into blockers, pursue, and gang tackle the ballcarrier.
- Make sure the appropriate drill personnel use the proper fundamentals and techniques of running, blocking, block shedding, and tackling.
- Enthusiasm and competition should be encouraged.

Safety Considerations:

- It is imperative that proper warm-up precede this drill.
- The adjacent drill participants should be instructed to remain alert.
- The coach should watch for and eliminate all unacceptable matchups as to size and athletic ability.
- The coach should monitor closely the intensity of the drill.
- A quick whistle is imperative with this drill.
- The training staff should be placed on special alert.

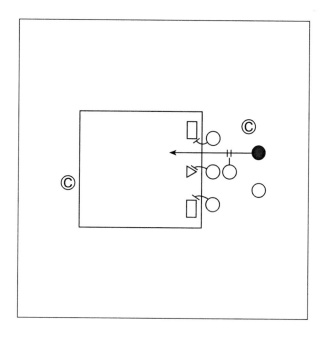

DRILL #81: THREE-ON-THREE

Lou L. Holtz
The College of William and Mary, North Carolina State University,
New York Jets, University of Arkansas, University of Minnesota,
University of Notre Dame, University of South Carolina
Overall Record: 236-123-7
National Champions: Notre Dame 1988
National Coach of the Year: Arkansas 1977; Notre Dame 1988

Objective: To teach and practice the proper fundamentals and techniques of the inside running game as they relate to both offense and defense. Incorporated are skills related to blocking for offensive linemen and tight ends, reading blocks and running for daylight for running backs, handoffs for quarterbacks, and defeating the blocker, pursuit, and tackling for defensive personnel.

Equipment Needed: Four cones and footballs

Description:

- Mark off an 8-by-10 drill area on the football field using existing yard lines and four cones (see diagram).
- Align an offense (three blockers, a quarterback, and two running backs) at the midpoint of the designated starting point of the drill area. If a center is among the three blockers, he lines up in the middle and over a football. If there is not a center, the quarterback holds the football at the center-quarterback exchange position (see diagram).
- Position three defensive players (linemen, defensive ends, or linebackers) nose-on-nose across from the three offensive blockers.
- Other drill participants stand adjacent to the drill area and yell encouragement to their teammates.
- The coach stands behind the defense and signals to the offense the snap count and the dive play to run.
- On the quarterback's cadence and snap count, the offense executes the designated dive play. The defensive personnel react, pursue, and tackle the ballcarrier.
- The offense is given three downs in which to cover the 10 yards for the score. When each play is completed, the football is placed at the point where the ballcarrier was tackled and midway between the two side boundaries. After a score or three downs, all personnel are rotated.
- The drill continues until all the drill participants have had a sufficient number of repetitions.

Coaching Points:

- Always check to see that all the personnel are aligned correctly and are in their proper stances.
- Playside blockers are instructed to drive the defenders straight off the football and the other two blockers execute drive blocks across the playside numbers of the defenders.
- Emphasize the importance of maintaining all blocks.
- Instruct runners to run tough and for daylight.
- Defenders are instructed to defeat their blockers, find and pursue the football, and gang tackle the ballcarrier.
- Outside defensive personnel should squeeze the play to the inside while keeping the outside arm free.
- Make sure the appropriate drill personnel use the proper fundamentals and techniques of running, blocking, block shedding, and tackling.
- Enthusiasm and competition should be encouraged.

Safety Considerations:

- It is imperative that proper warm-up precede this drill.
- The adjacent drill participants should be instructed to remain alert.
- The coach should watch for and eliminate all unacceptable matchups as to size and athletic ability.
- The coach should monitor closely the intensity of the drill.
- A quick whistle is in imperative with this drill.
- The training staff should be placed on special alert.

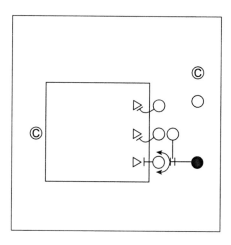

DRILL #82: WINNER'S PERIOD DRILL

Dr. Ted K. Kessinger
Bethany College
Overall Record: 208-50-1

Objective: To teach and practice the proper fundamentals and techniques of the running game as they relate to both goal line offense and defense.

Equipment Needed: Two cones and footballs

Description:

- Place two cones five-yards apart from the midpoint of the one-yard line.

- Align four offensive players (linemen and tight ends) between the two cones on the line of scrimmage.

- A running back, holding a football, is positioned three-yards behind and in the center of the four linemen.

- Align four defensive players (linemen and defensive ends) nose-on-nose across from the offensive linemen. One foot separates the offensive and defensive lines.

- A linebacker is positioned one-yard behind the defensive front and head-up on the running back.

- All other squad members surround the drill area and enthusiastically encourage their teammates.

- The quarterback stands adjacent to the drill area, and on his cadence and snap count, the offensive linemen drive out of their stances and block the defenders. The lone ballcarrier runs for the score. The two cones mark the outside parameters of the drill area.

- The defenders react to and defeat the blocks of the offense and pursue to tackle the ballcarrier.

- The drill continues for five minutes with the designated squad members taking turns.

Coaching Points:

- Always check to see that all the personnel are aligned correctly and are in their proper stances.

- Make sure that all the appropriate personnel practice the proper fundamentals and techniques of running, blocking, block shedding, and tackling.

- Enthusiasm and competition should be encouraged.
- This is not a coaching period and coaches should withhold their comments concerning corrections until after the drill is completed.

Safety Considerations:

- It is imperative that proper warm-up precede this drill.
- The adjacent drill participants should be instructed to remain alert.
- The coach should watch for and eliminate all unacceptable matchups as to size and athletic ability.
- The coach should monitor closely the intensity of the drill.
- A quick whistle is imperative with this drill.
- The training staff should be placed on special alert.

Variations:

- Can incorporate a lead blocker.
- Can incorporate a quarterback to take the snap from a center and execute a handoff.

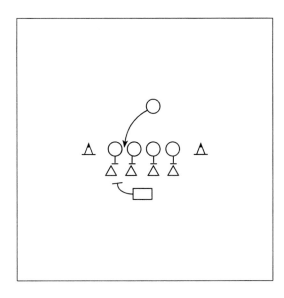

DRILL #83: WALK AWAY

John Gagliardi
Carroll College (MT), Saint John's University (MN)
Overall Record: 388-111-11
National Champions: St. John's 1963, 1965, and 1976
National Coach of the Year: St. John's 1965 and 1976

Objective: To teach and practice the mental and physical aspects of avoiding a retaliation (personal foul) penalty.

Equipment Needed: None

Description:

- Align a row of players five yards apart on a selected line of scrimmage.
- Align a second row of players five yards apart and two yards in front of and facing the players in the front row.
- On the coach's command, either one at a time or all together, players in a designated line step forward and strike a strong but controlled forearm blow or a two-handed push to the front-shoulder pad area of the front-facing opponent.
- The players receiving the blows must keep their composure and just *walk away*, thus avoiding a retaliation (personal foul) penalty.
- The drill continues until all the drill participants have had a sufficient number of repetitions.

Coaching Points:

- Instruct the players to only strike the opposing player in the shoulder-pad area.
- Discuss with the players the importance of keeping their composure, especially after receiving what they perceive as a late hit or *cheap shot* from an opposing player.
- The coach should point out a time when a retaliation penalty cost the team a touchdown or a victory.
- During film sessions, point out and praise examples of players *walking away* from a retaliation-penalty situation.

Safety Considerations:

- It is imperative that all controlled striking blows be delivered to the shoulder-pad area and never to the head area.
- The coach should monitor closely the intensity of the drill.

Variation:

- Can be conducted with the striking blow coming from behind the opponent and to the backside shoulder-pad area.

DRILL #84: HAT ON THE DUMMY

Dr. Frosty E. Westering
Pacific Lutheran University
Overall Record: 294-89-7
National Champions: 1980, 1987, 1993, and 1999
National Coach of the Year: 1983, 1993, and 1999

Objective: To teach and practice the proper fundamentals and techniques of offensive and defensive line play as it relates to pass blocking for the offensive linemen and pass rushing for defensive linemen.

Equipment Needed: Two stand-up dummies and two cones

Description:

- Align two half-line offensive lines (center, guard, and a tackle) on a selected line of scrimmage. The two offensive lines (one strongside and one weakside) should be separated by 10 yards (see diagram).

- Three defensive linemen are positioned head-up over each of the offensive linemen.

- Other drill participants stand adjacent to the drill area.

- A stand up dummy, with a cone placed on top (the hat) is placed seven-yards behind each of the centers.

- A coach is positioned behind the defender and designates the snap count for the offensive line by holding up one, two, or three fingers.

- On the coach's cadence and snap count, the designated offensive lineman (only one each from both offensive lines) executes their pass block as the designated defender drives by the block of the offensive lineman and attempts to knock the cone (hat) off the stand-up dummy.

- The coach blows the whistle after four seconds ending the drill. If the offensive lineman prevents the defender from knocking the cone (hat) off the dummy, he is successful. If not, the defensive lineman is successful.

- The drill continues until all the drill participants have had a sufficient number of repetitions.

Coaching Points:

- Always check to see that the linemen are aligned correctly and are in their proper stances.

- Make sure that all the offensive linemen practice the proper fundamentals and techniques of pass blocking and that defensive linemen stay in their proper pass-rush lanes and execute their designated pass-rush technique correctly.
- Insist that the drill be conducted at full speed.

Safety Considerations:

- Proper warm-up should precede the drill.
- The drill area should be clear of all foreign articles.
- The coach should monitor closely the intensity of the drill.
- Instruct the pass blocker to never *cut block* the pass rusher.
- The coach should watch for and eliminate all unacceptable matchups as to size and athletic ability.

Variations:

- Can be used as an enthusiastic and competitive drill by keeping a team score as to the number of successes achieved by the offense and defense.
- Can incorporate a fullback blocking a defensive end rushing.

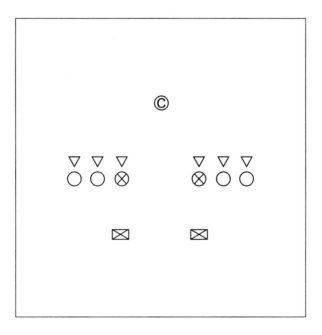

DRILL #85: PURSUIT DRILL

Dick Crum
Miami University (OH), University of North Carolina, Kent State University
Overall Record: 113-77-4

Objective: To teach and practice total team pursuit with special emphasis on reacting to the ball snap, getting off the ground, taking the proper pursuit angle, and maximum hustle.

Equipment Needed: Five cones, a football, and all available shields and dummies

Description:

- Align a seven-man offensive front, holding dummies, on a selected line of scrimmage.
- A defensive unit lines up over the offense.
- Other defensive units are positioned adjacent to the drill area.
- Lay all available shields and dummies at 45-degree angles on both sides of the defensive alignment (see diagram).
- A ballcarrier is positioned five-yards behind the offense.
- Five cones are placed at selected positions four-yards behind the offense (see diagram).
- The coach stands behind the defense and signals the offense as to the snap count and play direction.
- On the cadence and snap count, the offensive front steps playside with dummies in hand. The ballcarrier runs in and out of the cones and then sprints down the sideline.
- The defense reacts to the movement of the offensive personnel with the defensive linemen delivering blows to front-facing dummies, and then each defender executes a seat roll and pursues the ballcarrier.
- The drill continues with alternating defensive units pursuing both the left and right.

Coaching Points:

- Always check to see that all the personnel are aligned correctly and are in their proper stances.
- Make sure that all the defenders react correctly to the movement of the offense.
- Instruct all the defensive personnel as to their proper pursuit angles.

- Insist that all the personnel sprint to and touch the ballcarrier.

Safety Considerations:

- Proper warm-up should precede the drill.
- Instruct the pursuers only to tag the ballcarrier and not to abuse him.
- Players with knee problems should be excused from this drill.

Variations:

- Can be used with defensive secondary personnel executing backward pedal instead of the seat roll.
- Can have ballcarrier execute any number of running plays or even busted plays.
- Can have ballcarrier drop back to pass and try to scramble out of the pocket.

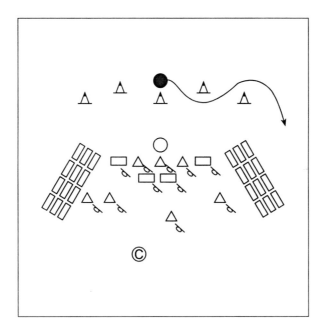

CHAPTER 14

Kicking Game

Drills

DRILL #86: BAD-SNAP DRILL FOR PUNTERS

Jackie W. Sherrill
Washington State University, University of Pittsburgh,
Texas A&M University, Mississippi State University
Overall Record: 175-101-4

Objective: To teach and practice the proper fundamentals and techniques of fielding and punting a poor center snap.

Equipment Needed: Footballs

Description:

- Place a football on the ground one foot in front of and to the right side of the punter.
- Position the punt-return personnel 55-yards downfield.
- Other punters stand adjacent to the drill area.
- At a deliberate pace, the punter steps laterally with his right foot first, picks up the football, and executes the punt.
- The drill continues with the football being placed on the ground one foot in front of and both to the left and right sides of the punter. (When the football is on the ground to the punter's left, he should take his lateral step with his left foot first.)
- The drill continues until the alternating punters have had a sufficient number of repetitions.

Coaching Points:

- Always check to see that the punters are in their proper stances.
- Instruct the punters always to step laterally first.
- Make sure the punters practice the proper mechanics in the execution of all punts.

Safety Considerations:

- Proper warm-up should precede the drill.
- The drill area should be clear of all foreign articles.

Variations:

- Can be used with the football turned sideways on the ground.
- Can be used with a passive punt rush.

- Can be used with alternating punters throwing the football to simulate poor center snaps (high, low, left, and right).
- Can be used as a punt-receiving drill.

DRILL #87: PUNTING RHYTHM AND SPEED DRILL

Robert J. "Bobby" Ross
The Citadel, University of Maryland, Georgia Tech,
San Diego Chargers, Detroit Lions
Overall Record: 171-144-2
National Champions: Georgia Tech 1990
National Coach of the Year: Georgia Tech 1990
National Football League Coach of the Year: San Diego 1992

Objective: To teach and practice the proper fundamentals of executing the long snap and punting the football.

Equipment Needed: Cone, stopwatch, and footballs

Description:

- Align a center over the football at the midpoint of the minus-15 yard line. Alternating centers stand adjacent to the snap area and may aid in the rotation of footballs.
- A punter stands with his heels on the goal line and directly behind the center. Alternating punters stand adjacent to the punting area and may be used to time *snap interval*. (Snap interval is defined as the time it takes for the snap to travel from the center's hands to the punter's hands.)
- The coach stands adjacent to the punting area and monitors the *release time* (Release time is defined as the time it takes for the punter to execute the punt after receiving the snap.)
- Position punt-return personnel 40-yards downfield. A cone is also placed 40-yards downfield and is used to judge the distance of each punt. A coach stands adjacent to punt-receiving area to monitor *hang time*.
- On the punter's cadence, the ball is snapped and the punt is executed.
- The drill continues until all the drill participants have had a sufficient number of repetitions.
- The drill should be run from various positions on the field.

Coaching Points:

- Always check to see that all the personnel are aligned correctly and are in their proper stances.
- Make sure the centers and punters practice the proper mechanics in the execution of their center snaps and punts respectively.

- The punters' release time should be 1.3 seconds or less. Snap-time intervals should be .8 seconds or less. Total release time should be 2.2 seconds or less (.1 margin of error).

Safety Considerations:

- Proper warm-up should precede the drill.
- The drill area should be clear of all foreign articles. This includes the sideline areas.

Variations:

- Can be used with other players harassing punters and snappers.
- Can be used with the coach simulating bad center snaps.
- Can be used as punt receiving drill.

DRILL #88: PUNT RETURN CONE DRILL

Willie E. Jeffries
High School, Wichita State University, Howard University,
South Carolina State University
Overall Record: 250-138-8
National Black College Champions:
South Carolina State 1976, 1977, and 1994; Howard 1987
National Black College Coach of the Year:
South Carolina State 1976 and 1977; Howard 1977

Objective: To teach and practice the proper fundamentals and techniques of defending the punt and setting up a sideline punt return.

Equipment Needed: Six cones and footballs

Description:

- Align a scout punting team over the football at the midpoint of a selected line of scrimmage.

- Place cones on an angle beginning on the field numbers 15-yards downfield from the line of scrimmage and extending five-yards inside the return-side hash mark. Five yards separate each cone (see diagram).

- Position a punt return team over the scout punting team.

- Coaches stand two-yards outside the return-side defensive end, inside the return-side hash mark 30 yards from the line of scrimmage, and adjacent to the punt returner.

- Alternating punt return units are positioned on the sideline.

- On the cadence and ball snap, the defensive ends rush the punter and the remaining front defenders hold up their front-facing opponents with a two-count hand shiver. After these assignments are executed, the front defenders position themselves in the sideline return wall. The defensive backs also move to their areas of responsibility with the return-side halfback setting the wall (see diagram). The punt returner is instructed to catch the punt and run behind the wall. The punter punts the football as the offensive personnel move to cover the punt.

- The preceding procedure is executed with each defender in turn jogging through his assignment.

- Repeat the preceding procedure with all the defenders jogging through their assignments as a unit.

- Repeat the preceding procedure several times at full speed.
- The drill continues with the sideline returns both left and right from various field positions.
- The drill may progress to live contact.

Coaching Points:

- Always check to see that all the personnel are aligned correctly and are in their proper stances.
- Instruct the defensive ends to force the punt before moving into wall.
- Insist that the remaining front five hold up their front-facing opponents for two counts. It is also imperative that these same defenders circle the coach stationed on the line of scrimmage before they move to form the punt return wall.
- The personnel who form the wall are reminded to keep a five-yard separation and to move back upfield as the punt returner moves past them in the wall.

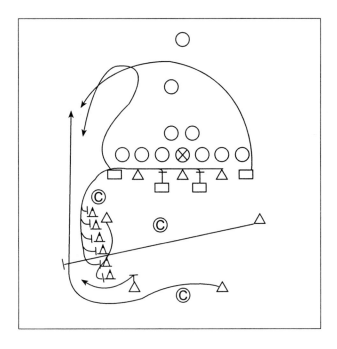

Safety Considerations:

- It is imperative that proper warm-up precede this drill.
- The drill area should be clear of all foreign articles. This includes the sideline areas.
- The drill should progress from jog-through to live contact.
- The coach should monitor closely the intensity of the drill.
- The drill should be executed live only under the most monitored conditions.
- When the drill is executed live, all the punt return personnel are reminded that all blocks must be executed above the waist.
- A quick whistle is imperative with this drill.

Variation:

- Can be used as a passive or live drill.

DRILL #89: REVERSE PUNT RETURN

William "Bill" Billings
Edenton Holmes High School (NC), Middletown High School (Del)
Overall Record: 233-51-9
North Carolina State Champions: 1954, 1956, 1957, and 1959
Delaware State Champions: 1964, 1965, 1966, 1970, and 1978

Objective: To teach and practice the proper execution of the reverse punt return from a twin-safety punt-return alignment.

Equipment Needed: Footballs and hand shields

Description:

- Position a punt team, holding hand shields, at the midpoint of a selected line of scrimmage.

- Position a twin-safety punt-return team in its designated punt-return alignment over the punt team.

- Prior to breaking the huddle, the punt-return team calls either a left or right sideline return.

- On the punter's cadence and snap count, the punt team executes a punt.

- The punt-return team reacts to the snap count and executes their various sideline return assignments as noted in the following five procedures (see diagram):

  □ The defensive linemen execute a two-count hand shiver on their front-facing opponent and then move to set up the outside wall for the designated sideline return (see diagram).

  □ The backside defensive end rushes the punter to ensure that the punt is executed. He then moves to take his position in the outside wall.

  □ The defensive linebackers impede any fast covering punt-team coverage personnel and then move to set up the inside wall for the designated sideline return (see diagram).

  □ The cornerbacks align themselves, head-up the outside coverage personnel (gunners) and impede their downfield progress, keeping them off the punt returners.

  □ The twin safeties set up in their normal punt-return alignments. As one safety catches the punt, the other safety positions himself at a point behind and adjacent to the punt receiver. In unison and determined by the designated sideline return, they either fake or execute the handoff.

- The drill continues until the desired number of both left and right sideline returns have been executed.

Coaching Points:

- Always check to see that all the punt-return personnel are aligned correctly and are in their proper stances.
- Insist that all the front-facing linemen execute their hand shiver before moving to set up in the outside wall.
- Make sure the cornerbacks impede the progress of the outside gunners.
- Insist that the twin safeties execute the fake or handoff in a manner that will deceive the punt-coverage personnel. It is imperative that the safety not having the football carries out a convincing fake.

Safety Considerations:

- Proper warm-up should precede the drill.
- The drill area should be clear of all foreign articles. This includes the sideline areas.
- The drill should be conducted live only under the most monitored conditions.
- Always remind the punt-return personnel that blocks must always be executed above the opponent's waist.

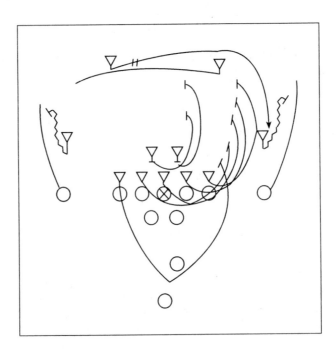

DRILL #90: PUNT BLOCK

R.C. Slocum
Texas A&M University
Overall Record: 117-41-2

Objective: To teach and practice the proper fundamentals and techniques in blocking a punt with special emphasis on identifying the block spot.

Equipment Needed: Footballs

Description:

- Align a scout-spread punt team on a selected line of scrimmage. (You may substitute cones in the place of punting personnel.)

- Align an eight-man defensive front in their designated punt-blocking positions facing the punting team.

- Designate the *block spot* at a point nine yards directly behind the center. (Mark the *block spot* with a dot.)

- A punter with football in hand is positioned 10-yards deep so that his punting foot will be directly over the *block spot*, as he takes only one step before punting the football.

- On the punter's cadence and snap count, the center with a football at the *snap ready* position simulates the center snap.

- Beginning with the defender on the far left, each defensive player, in turn, drives out of his stance on the simulated snap of the center and runs through the *passive* block of the offensive player. He then sprints for the *block spot* and blocks the punt as it comes off the punter's foot.

- The drill continues until all the defenders have had a sufficient number of repetitions in blocking a punt.

Coaching Points:

- Always check to see that all the defenders are aligned correctly and are in their proper stances.

- Instruct the punt blockers to read the simulated snap of the center and to get a jump on the ball snap.

- Stress the importance of accelerating though the *block spot*.

- Instruct the punt blockers to focus their eye on the football and to catch it as it comes off the punter's foot.

- Instruct the punter to take only one step, striking the ball at less than half tempo, and to always contact the ball over the *block spot*.

Safety Considerations:

- Proper warm-up should precede the drill.
- Helmets should be worn and chinstraps snapped.
- The coach should monitor closely the intensity of the drill.
- It is imperative that all the punt blockers avoid all contact with the punter.

Variation:

- Can be used as a *scoop and score* drill by designated a trailing punt blocker to scoop up the football after the block.

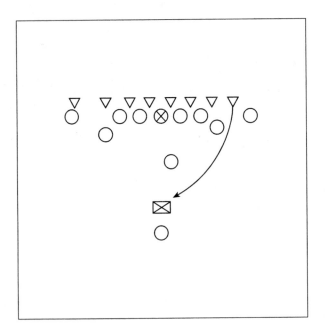

DRILL #91: PUNT PROTECTION

"Mel" Tjeerdsma
Austin College, Northwest Missouri State University
Overall Record: 136-63-4
National Champions: Northwest Missouri 1998 and 1999
National Coach of the Year: Northwest Missouri 1998 and 1999

Objective: To teach and practice the proper fundamentals and techniques of protecting the punter from the spread-punt formation.

Equipment Needed: Footballs

Description:

- Align a strongside spread-punt formation (center, guard, tackle, wingman, personal protector, and punter) in their normal positions on the right hash mark of the 50-yard line. A duplicate weakside spread-punt formation is aligned on the left hash mark. Ten yards should separate the two formations (see diagram).

- Align a half-line five-man defensive punt-blocking team in front of each half-line punt team.

- On the punter's cadence and snap count, the designated punt-team personnel execute their punt-protection blocks against the onrushing punt-blocking team.

- The drill continues until both strongside and weakside punting personnel have had a sufficient number of repetitions.

Coaching Points:

- Always check to see that all the punting personnel are aligned correctly and are in their proper stances.

- After the center, guards, tackles, and wingmen have identified their blocking assignments, instruct them to neutralize the defenders by delivering a two-hand palms-up blow to the numbers.

- Instruct the center, guards, tackles, and wingmen to keep their shoulders squared to the line of scrimmage as they execute a three-step punt-blocking technique (inside foot, outside foot, and inside foot).

- Remind all the punt protectors that the key to man-on-man punt protection is to allow the punt rushers to gain lateral movement but not forward movement.

Safety Considerations:

- Proper warm-up should precede the drill.
- The drill area should be clear of all foreign articles.
- The drill should progress from form blocking to live blocking.
- Instruct the punt rushers not to run into or rough the punter.

Variation:

- Can be used as a full-team spread-punt protection drill aligned against an 8-, 9-, or 10-man defensive front.

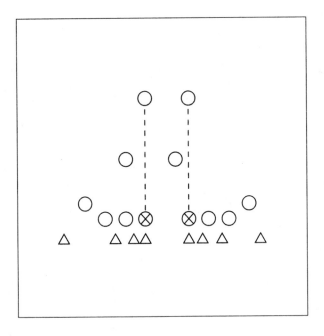

CHAPTER 15

General Agility

Drills

DRILL #92: BULLNECK DRILL

Wayne "Woody" Hayes (Deceased)
Denison University, Miami University (OH), The Ohio State University
Overall Record: 238-72-10
National Champions: Ohio State 1954, 1957, 1961, 1968, and 1970
National Coach of the Year: Ohio State 1957, 1968, and 1975
College Football Hall of Fame: 1983
Amos Alonzo Stagg Award: 1986
AFCA President: 1963

Objective: To stretch and strengthen the muscles of the neck.

Equipment Needed: None

Description:

- Align all the squad members in calisthenics lines.
- The drill coordinator is positioned in front of the team.
- On the drill coordinator's command, all players pair up on pre-designated yard lines. One of the paired players is positioned on his hands and knees facing the drill coordinator. The other partner stands adjacent to him.
- On the drill coordinator's command, the standing player places his clasped hands behind the head of his partner. From this position, an isometric contraction is executed for five to eight seconds with the down partner's head resisting the pulling forward action of his partner.
- The procedure is repeated with the standing player pushing against the right and then the left sides of his partner's head with the palms of his hands.
- Now the standing player clasps his hands under the chin of his partner and pulls upward. The down-drill participant again offers strong resistance.
- The drill participants now change places and the procedures are repeated.

Coaching Points:

- Instruct all the drill participants to start and stop all procedures on the drill coordinator's commands.
- Insist that all down-drill participants hold their heads *way up* as high as they can get it.

Safety Considerations:

- The pressure exerted by the standing partner never should be great enough to force his partner's head out of its original position.
- The pressure applied by the standing partner should be increased gradually from day to day.

DRILL #93: FOUR-CORNER DRILL

Glenn "Bo" Schembechler
Miami University (OH), University of Michigan
Overall Record: 234-65-8
National Coach of the Year: Michigan 1969 and 1977
College Football Hall of Fame: 1993
Amos Alonzo Stagg Award: 1999
AFCA President: 1983

Objective: To develop general agility, flexibility, quickness, coordination, and reaction.

Equipment Needed: Four cones

Description:

- Align four cones five-yards apart in a square (see diagram).
- Position the drill participants in a straight line behind one of the cones.
- The coach stands adjacent to the start-finish area.
- On the coach's command, the first drill participant drives out of his stance and *bear crawls* to the first cone. He then stands up and faces the outside of the drill area and *cariocas* to the second cone. He now *runs backward* to the third cone, and then turns and *sprints* past the fourth cone.
- The drill continues until all the drill participants have had a sufficient number of repetitions.
- The drill should be conducted in both clockwise and counterclockwise directions.

Coaching Points:

- Always check to see that all the personnel start the drill in their proper stances.
- Instruct the drill participants to get their arms and legs up under them when they execute the *bear crawl.*
- Make sure the players maintain the desired body positions throughout the drill.
- Insist that the drill be conducted at full speed.
- Instruct the drill participants to sprint past the fourth cone.

Safety Considerations:

- Proper warm-up should precede the drill.
- Maintain a minimum distance of five-yards between performing drill participants.

- Instruct all the personnel as to the proper techniques of executing the *bear crawl* and *carioca*.

- The players with knee problems should be excused from the *carioca* and backward run portions of this drill.

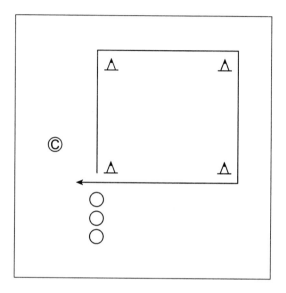

DRILL #94: MIRROR DRILL

Paul F. Dietzel
Louisiana State University, United States Military Academy,
University of South Carolina
Overall Record: 115-88-4
National Champions: Louisiana State 1958
National Coach of the Year: Louisiana State 1958
AFCA President: 1969

Objective: To develop general agility, quickness, coordination, and reaction time. Incorporated are skills related to recovering a fumble.

Equipment Needed: Footballs

Description:

- Align a ballcarrier, holding a football, in a front-facing position toward two pursuing players. Five yards separate the ballcarrier from the first pursuer. The second pursuer lines up three-yards behind the first (see diagram).

- This drill alignment can be repeated at various positions on the field.

- On the coach's command, the ballcarrier moves quickly either to his left or right, while the two pursuers mirror his moves while maintaining a squared-shoulder relationship to him.

- The ballcarrier continues with various movement patterns including forward and sideward rolls in an attempt to lose the pursuers.

- Finally, after four to six movement patterns have been executed, the ballcarrier fumbles the football and moves clear.

- The pursuers yell *ball - ball* and move to recover the loose football.

- The drill continues until all the drill participants have had a sufficient number of repetitions both as ballcarriers and as pursuers.

Coaching Points:

- Insist that all the pursuers keep their shoulders squared to the ballcarrier at all times.

- Instruct ballcarriers to make short, abrupt changes in direction.

Safety Considerations:

- Proper warm-up should precede the drill.
- Maintain a safe distance between the three drill participants.
- Instruct all personnel as to the proper techniques of recovering a fumble.
- Instruct the first pursuer to the fumbled football to make the recovery with the second pursuer assigned to protect him.
- If the players are not in full gear, do not execute the fumble and fumble recovery.

Variation:

- Encourage the ballcarriers to use their imagination in trying to elude the pursuers.

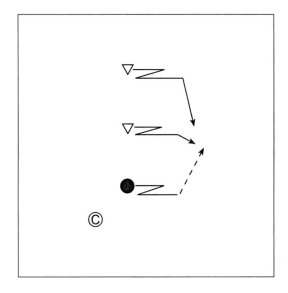

DRILL #95: WAVE DRILL

Charles "Cholly Mac" McClendon (Deceased)
Louisiana State University
Overall Record: 137-59-7
National Coach of the Year: 1970
College Football Hall of Fame: 1986
Amos Alonzo Stagg Award: 1992
AFCA President: 1979
AFCA Executive Director: 1982-1994

Objective: To develop general agility, concentration, reaction, body control, sense of direction, and competitiveness. Incorporated are skills related to recovering a fumble.

Equipment Needed: Footballs

Description:

- Align two players in a *football position* five-yards apart on the five-yard line. Players face the sideline.
- A third player designated the leader stands five yards in front and faces the two players designated the followers (see diagram).
- The left and right boundaries of the drill area are the goal line and 10-yard line.
- Other drill participants stand on the sideline.
- The coach stands adjacent to the drill area with a football in hand.
- On the coach's command, the leader executes various movement patterns including cross-over steps left and right, side rolls left and right, squats, ground touches, jumps into air with arms raised over head, and forward rolls (forward rolls should be executed vertically to the five-yard line).
- The followers try to mirror the exact movement patterns of the leader while maintaining a nose-to-nose relationship to him.
- The drill is concluded when the coach pitches the football outside the drill area and yells *ball - ball*. All the drill participants now try to recover the loose football.
- The drill continues until all the drill participants have had a sufficient number of repetitions as both leaders and followers.

Coaching Points:

- Insist that all the followers keep their shoulders squared to an imaginary line of scrimmage throughout the drill.

- Instruct all the drill participants to execute their movement patterns as quickly as possible.
- This should be a fun drill done by all positions.
- This drill is not recommended as a conditioning drill.

Safety Considerations:

- Proper warm-up should precede the drill.
- Maintain a minimum distance of five-yards between each of the three drill participants.
- Instruct all the personnel as to the proper techniques of recovering a fumble.
- The coach should monitor closely the intensity of the fumble recovery.

Variation:

- If players are not in full gear, a breakdown and a sprint out are substituted for the fumble recovery.

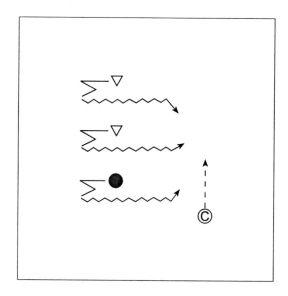

DRILL #96: FOUR AND TWO

Clarence Stasavich (Deceased)
[Drill submitted by David M. Alexander]
Lenoir-Rhyne College, East Carolina University
Overall Record: 170-64-8
National Champions: Lenoir-Rhyne 1960
National Coach of the Year: Lenoir-Rhyne 1959; East Carolina 1964

Objective: To teach and practice various movement patterns and methods of catching the football. Incorporated are skills related to reaction, agility, and quickness.

Equipment Needed: Footballs

Description:

- Align the drill participants in a row perpendicular to a selected line of scrimmage.
- A quarterback, holding a football, is positioned 15 yards in front of the first drill participants (see diagram).
- On the quarterback's command, the first drill participant assumes the football position.
- On the quarterback's ball signal (shows pass), the first drill participant takes four-steps up and two-steps back and then cuts a 90-degree angle either left or right on quarterback's shoulder turn.
- The quarterback throws the pass to the drill participant who makes the interception and returns the football to the quarterback.
- The drill continues until all the drill participants have had a sufficient number of repetitions.
- The drill can be conducted with any number of drill stations.

Coaching Points:

- Insist that the drill participants maintain good body alignment throughout the drill.
- Instruct the drill participants to always watch the quarterback.
- Insist that the drill be conducted at full speed.

Safety Considerations:

- Proper warm-up should precede the drill.
- The drill area should be clear of all foreign articles.

- If more than one drill station is used, a minimum distance of 25 yards should be maintained between stations.

Variations:

- Can be used with the drill participants moving back at a 45-degree angle after they have completed their four-up and two-back stepping.
- Can be used with the drill participants executing a backpedal after their four-up, two-back, and 90-degree cut either left or right stepping.

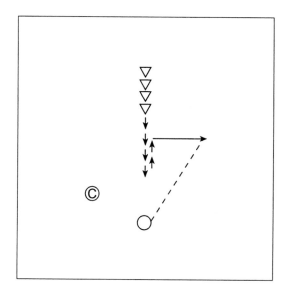

DRILL #97: CONE DRILL

Howard L. Schnellenberger
University of Miami, University of Louisville, The University of Oklahoma,
Baltimore Colts, Florida Atlantic University
Overall Record: 108-96-3
National Champions: University of Miami 1983
National Coach of the Year: University of Miami 1983

Objective: To teach and practice the proper fundament of various movements related to football. Incorporated are skills related to reaction, agility, and quickness.

Equipment Needed: Four cones

Description:

- Place four cones seven-yards apart to form a square.
- Position the drill participants in a straight line next to cone A as shown in the diagram.
- The drill is conducted in four phases and in a counterclockwise direction as noted in the following. The coach stands inside the square during the first two phases of the drill, and then moves outside the cones for the last two phases.
  - *Shuffle.* On the coach's command, the first drill participant assumes the *football position* facing cone A. On the coach's second command, he shuffles to cone B and executes a 90-clegree left turn and sprints past cone C. The drill continues with the other drill participants taking their turns. The players now return to cone B.
  - *Step Around.* On the coach's command, the first drill participant assumes a three-point stance beside cone B and faces the outside of the drill area. On the coach's second command, he steps and pivots to the left touching cone B with his left hand. The drill participant now sprints to cone C, keeping his eyes on the coach who is still positioned inside the square. The drill continues with the other drill participants taking their turns.
  - *Backpedal.* On the coach's command, the first drill participant assumes the *football position* beside cone C with his back to cone D. The coach moves outside the drill area and takes a front-facing position to the drill participant. The coach now attempts to place his hands on the drill participant's head. The drill participant reacts to the coach's hand movement and sprints backward past cone D. The drill continues with the other drill participants sprinting backward.

- □ *Scramble.* On the coach's command, the first drill participant assumes a three-point stance beside cone D and faces cone A. The coach is positioned midway between the two cones and faces the drill participant. On the coach's command, the drill participant sprints to the coach and then scrambles on *all fours* past cone A. The drill continues with other drill participants taking their turns.

- The four phases of the drill are now executed in a clockwise direction.

Coaching Points:

- Always check to see that the drill participants are in the correct *football position* or in their proper stances.

- In executing the *shuffle,* make sure that the drill participants keep their shoulders square to the cones and avoid crossover stepping.

- Make sure that all the drill participants keep their eyes on the coach as they execute the *step around* phase of the drill.

A

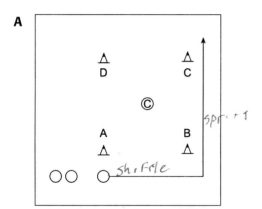

B

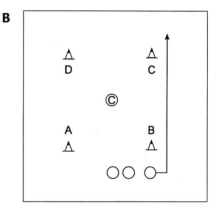

C

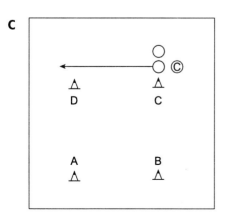

D

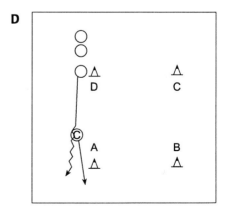

- In executing the *backpedal*, instruct the drill participants to use short, choppy steps and to keep the head up. They should also avoid false stepping as they initiate the backward run.
- Insist that the drill participants explode out of their stances and sprint to the coach before executing the *scramble*.
- Insist that the drill be conducted at full speed.

Safety Considerations:

- Proper warm-up should precede the drill.
- Players with knee problems should be excused from certain phases of this drill.

Variation:

- Can be used as an offensive line drill.

CHAPTER 16

Drills for Developing and Maintaining

Cardiovascular Endurance

DRILL #98: FELLOWSHIP

S. S. "Red" Wilson
High School, Elon University, Duke University
Overall Record: 226-99-14

Objective: To develop or maintain a desired level of cardiovascular endurance and to build team morale.

Equipment Needed: Stopwatch

Description:

- Align all the squad members flat on their backs with their feet toward the middle of a *fellowship* circle.
- The drill coordinator is positioned in the middle of the *fellowship* circle with a stopwatch and whistle.
- Other coaches are placed at various positions among squad members and serve as motivators.
- The drill is conducted in four phases (four quarters).
  - First quarter: On the drill coordinator's whistle, all the squad members begin doing sit-ups at as fast as possible. After 15 seconds, the drill coordinator blows his whistle again and all squad members turn over on their stomachs as quickly as possible to a push-up position. (Heads are facing center of circle.) On a third whistle, all the drill participants begin doing push-ups. After a 15-second push-up period, the first phase (first quarter) is concluded.
  - Second quarter: Repeat the first quarter procedure. At the conclusion of this quarter, rest for 20 seconds (half time).
  - Third and fourth quarters: Repeat the first and second quarters.

Coaching Points:

- Make sure all the drill participants execute their sit-ups and push-ups correctly.
- Insist that all the squad members execute their sit-ups and push-ups as fast as possible.
- Encourage all the drill participants to *whoop it up* during the entire drill.
- Coaches should yell words of encouragement to motivate the players.

Safety Considerations:

- Proper warm-up should precede the drill.
- Coaches should monitor closely the fatigue level of all the drill participants throughout the drill period.
- The training staff should be placed on special alert.
- The drill should not be conducted during extreme heat or high humidity conditions.

Variations:

- Recommended for pre-season only.
- Can substitute sprints during morning practice.
- Can vary sit-up and push-up time intervals.

DRILL #99: 300-YARD SHUTTLE RUN

William "Mack" Brown
Appalachian State University, Tulane University,
University of North Carolina, University of Texas
Overall Record: 124-87-1

Objective: To test for and develop or maintain a desired level of cardiovascular endurance. Incorporated are skills related to agility and quickness. The test can be administered on the summer reporting date and at the conclusion of the winter conditioning program. Time-interval standards for the shuttle run are correlated with the individual's 40-time (4.6-40–under 46.0 second shuttle run; 5.2-40–under 52.0 shuttle run, etc.).

Equipment Needed: Stopwatch and four cones

Description:

- Align two cones five-yards apart from the midpoint of a selected goal line. Two additional cones are placed in corresponding positions on the 50-yard line.

- All the drill participants are positioned adjacent to the start area on the goal line.

- One coach is placed near the goal line and one on the 50-yard line.

- On the goal line coach's command, the first drill participant takes a stance behind starting line and sprints to and touches the 50-yard line and returns to the goal line. Procedure is repeated until drill participant has covered 300 yards.

- The goal line coach monitors each drill participant's time and starts his watch on the runner's first movement.

- The drill continues until all the drill participants have run a sufficient number of 300-yard shuttle runs.

Coaching Points:

- Insist that all the drill participants begin each shuttle run from behind the goal line and run through and touch all designated turn-around points.

- Make sure that all the runners run past the finish line.

- All the runners should be encouraged to use fundamentally sound principles of running.

Safety Considerations:

- Proper warm-up should precede the drill.
- The drill area should be clear of all foreign articles.
- Coaches should monitor closely the fatigue level of all the drill participants throughout the drill period.
- The training staff should be placed on special alert.
- It is imperative that each drill participant be given a five-minute rest period after he has concluded his shuttle run.
- The drill should not be conducted during extreme heat or high humidity conditions.

Variation:

- Can have two or more drill participants run course at the same time.

DRILL #100: TEAM-KICKOFF CONDITIONING

Ronald "Ron" Randleman
William Penn College, Pittsburg State University, Sam Houston State University
Overall Record: 202-147-6
National Coach of the Year: Pittsburg State 1981

Objective: To develop or maintain a desired level of cardiovascular endurance while teaching the basics of covering a kickoff.

Equipment Needed: 10 cones, kicking tee, and a football

Description:

- Place ten cones on a football field representing the pre-kickoff return alignment of a receiving kickoff team. Kickoff returners are aligned in their normal kickoff-return position at the goal line.

- Position the number one kickoff-coverage team in its regular kickoff alignment. All other players with the exception of offensive linemen line up behind the first kickoff team.

- On the coach's whistle, the kicker executes the kickoff and the number one kickoff-coverage team sprints full speed downfield covering the kick.

- The first kick returner catches the football and returns it approximately 10-yards upfield in a designated direction and then comes to a stop.

- All the kickoff coverage personnel continue sprinting through their designated coverage lanes and then *squeeze* down on the kick returner. As the kickoff team approaches the kick returner, all the coverage personnel break down in the basic football position *buzzing* their feet.

- On the coach's command, the coverage team sprints to the near sideline and the kick returner sprints upfield for the touchdown.

- The kickoff-coverage team now jogs back down the sideline and prepares for their next kickoff coverage. The kick returner does the same.

- The drill continues until all the drill participants have had a sufficient number of repetitions.

Coaching Points:

- Always check to see that all the kickoff-coverage personnel are aligned correctly and are in their proper stances.

- Insist that all the kickoff-coverage personnel sprint through their designated coverage lane before *squeezing* down on the kick returner.
- Make sure that all the kickoff-coverage personnel break down in the basic football position and *buzz* their feet as they *squeeze* down on the kick returner.
- Instruct the kick returner to sprint toward the goal line after the kickoff-coverage personnel sprint to the near sideline.

Safety Considerations:

- Proper warm-up should precede the drill.
- The drill area should be clear of all foreign articles. This includes both the sideline areas.
- The drill should not be conducted during extreme heat or high humidity conditions.
- The coach and training staff should monitor closely the fatigue level of all the drill participants throughout the drill period.

Variation:

- Can be used as a kickoff-coverage drill.

DRILL #101: SHUTTLE RUN

Bill Snyder
Kansas State University
Overall Record: 105-49-1
National Coach of the Year: 1994 and 1998

Objective: To test for a desired level of cardiovascular endurance. Incorporated are skills related to running and changing directions.

Equipment Needed: Cones, stopwatches, notepads, and pencils

Description:

- Lay out a shuttle-running lane by placing two cones five-yards apart on a selected line of scrimmage, and two additional cones five-yards apart and 60-yards downfield. More shuttle lanes can be formed as necessary. (Eight shuttle lanes are recommended.)

- All the drill participants are positioned behind the start of the shuttle-running lanes.

- Coaches are positioned at each of the starting positions and serve as starters. Two additional coaches with stopwatches and a third coach who serves as a recorder are positioned at the finish line.

- On the starting coach's command, the first drill participant in each shuttle lane drives out of his stance and sprints from one end of the shuttle run to the other until 300 yards have been covered. (5x60 yards=300 yards)

- After completing the first shuttle run, each drill participant walks back to the starting line and is allowed a one-minute rest period before performing a second and final shuttle run.

- It is recommended that the average time of the two shuttle runs be equal to or below the drill participant's 40-yard sprint time multiplied by 10. (Example: If a player runs a 4.5 40-yard sprint, the average time of his two shuttle runs should be 45 seconds, because 4.5x10=45.)

Coaching Points:

- Insist that all the drill participants begin each shuttle run behind the designated starting point and in a designated stance.

- All the drill participants should be encouraged to use fundamentally sound principles of running.

- The emphasis should be placed on getting a good start.

- Instruct all the drill participants to touch, but not cross over, each ending line. They should not slow down in the turns, but enter each turn low making a half turn while touching the end line with the lead foot and then accelerating while completing the turn around.

- Instruct the drill participants that while both shuttle runs should be at near full speed, the first run should be at a pace two to four seconds faster than the required average time of the two shuttle runs. (Example: if a player runs a 4.5 40-yard sprint, his first shuttle run should be 45 seconds minus two to four seconds. His second shuttle run can be two to four seconds slower than the first run.)

Safety Considerations:

- Proper warm-up should precede the drill.
- The drill area should be clear of all foreign articles.
- The drill should not be conducted during extreme heat or high humidity conditions.
- The training staff should be placed on full alert.
- The coach and training staff should monitor closely the fatigue level of all the drill participants throughout the drill.
- A complete physical examination should precede all preseason cardiovascular-conditioning testing.

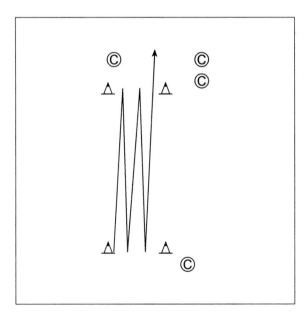

APPENDICES

101 Legends of the Game

Name	Team**	W*	L*	T*	%	Drill #
Akers, Fred	Purdue	113	82	3	0.5783	11
Alvarez, Barry	Wisconsin	84	55	4	0.6014	76
Ault, Chris	Nevada	163	63	1	0.7203	62
Beamer, Frank	Virginia Tech	149	88	4	0.6266	55
Billings, Bill	Holmes High School	253	51	9	0.8227	89
Bowden, Bobby	Florida State	323	91	4	0.7775	22
Brown, Mack	Texas	124	87	1	0.5873	99
Broyles, Chuck	Pittsburg State	123	23	2	0.8378	40
Broyles, J. Frank	Arkansas	142	62	6	0.6905	9
Bruce, Earle	Colorado State	154	90	2	0.6301	79
Bryant, Bear (D)	Alabama	323	85	17	0.7800	32
Butterfield, Jim	Ithaca	206	71	1	0.7428	46
Carpenter, Gene	Millersville	220	90	6	0.7057	35
Casanova, Len (D)	Oregon	104	97	10	0.5166	73
Christopherson, Jim	Concordia-Moorhead	218	101	7	0.6794	27
Claiborne, Jerry (D)	Kentucky	179	122	8	0.5922	80
Cooper, John	Ohio State	193	83	6	0.6950	52
Cozza, Carm	Yale	179	119	5	0.5990	53
Crum, Dick	Kent State	113	77	4	0.5928	85
Daugherty, Duffy (D)	Michigan State	109	69	5	0.6093	59
DeBerry, Fisher	Air Force	141	78	1	0.6432	43
Devaney, Bob (D)	Nebraska	136	30	7	0.8064	3
Dietzel, Paul	South Carolina	115	88	4	0.5652	94
Donahue, Terry	UCLA	151	74	8	0.6652	6
Dooley, Vince	Georgia	201	77	10	0.7153	51
Dooley, William	Wake Forest	162	126	5	0.5614	18
Dye, Pat	Auburn	153	62	5	0.7068	65
Edwards, LaVell	Brigham Young	257	101	3	0.7161	24

(D) = Deceased
* As of May 31, 2002
** Last team coached in most cases. Some teams selected based on other criteria.

Name	Team**	W*	L*	T*	%	Drill #
Farley, Dick	Williams	101	16	3	0.8542	29
Faurot, Don (D)	Missouri	163	93	13	0.6301	8
Ford, Bob	Albany	180	130	2	0.5801	25
Franchione, Dennis	Alabama	145	70	2	0.6728	19
Fry, J. Hayden	Iowa	232	178	10	0.5643	34
Fulmer, Phillip	Tennessee	95	20	0	0.8261	12
Gagliardi, John	St. John's (MN)	388	111	11	0.7716	83
Gailey, Chan	Georgia Tech	54	36	1	0.5989	54
Gaither, Alonzo (D)	Florida A&M	203	36	4	0.8436	15
Girardi, Frank	Lycoming	226	69	5	0.7617	30
Glenn, Joe	Montana	147	56	1	0.7230	38
Green, Dennis	Minnesota Vikings	123	125	0	0.4960	67
Harring, Roger	Wisconsin-La Crosse	261	74	8	0.7726	28
Hatfield, Ken	Rice	155	108	4	0.5880	33
Hayes, Woody (D)	Ohio State	238	72	10	0.7594	92
Holtz, Lou	South Carolina	236	123	7	0.6544	81
Howard, Frank (D)	Clemson	165	118	12	0.5797	78
James, Don	Washington	178	76	3	0.6984	56
Jeffries, Willie	South Carolina State	250	138	8	0.6414	88
Joe, Billy	Florida A&M	221	89	4	0.7102	37
Johnson, Jimmy	Miami Dolphins	171	102	2	0.6255	69
Kehres, Larry	Mount Union	178	17	3	0.9066	47
Kelly, Mike	Dayton	195	40	1	0.8284	74
Kessinger, Ted	Bethany	208	50	1	0.8050	82
Kidd, Roy	Eastern Kentucky	307	119	8	0.7166	39
MacPherson, Dick	Syracuse	110	94	5	0.5383	66
Majors, John	Pittsburgh	185	137	10	0.5723	49
Mallory, Bill	Indiana	168	129	4	0.5648	68
Manlove Jr., Bill	LaSalle	212	110	1	0.6579	41
Maurer, Dave	Wittenberg	129	23	3	0.8419	4
McCartney, Bill	Colorado	93	55	5	0.6242	71
McClendon, Charles (D)	LSU	137	59	7	0.6951	95
McKay, John (D)	Southern Cal	171	128	9	0.5698	1
Mudra, Darrell	Northern Iowa	200	81	4	0.7088	48
Murray, Bill (D)	Duke	213	77	14	0.7237	72
Nehlen, Don	West Virginia	202	112	6	0.6406	36
Osborne, Tom	Nebraska	255	49	3	0.8355	20
Parseghian, Ara	Notre Dame	170	58	6	0.7393	75

Name	Team**	W*	L*	T*	%	Drill #
Paterno, Joe	Penn State	327	96	3	0.7711	16
Randleman, Ron	Sam Houston	202	147	6	0.5775	100
Raymond, Tubby	Delaware	300	119	3	0.7145	14
Reade, Bob	Augustana	289	44	5	0.8624	63
Robinson, Eddie	Grambling	408	165	15	0.7066	77
Ross, Bobby	Detroit Lions	171	144	2	0.5426	87
Royal, Darrell	Texas	196	64	5	0.7491	70
Schembechler, Bo	Michigan	234	65	8	0.7752	93
Schipper, Ron	Central Iowa	320	78	5	0.8002	64
Schnellenberger, Howard	Florida Atlantic	108	96	3	0.5290	97
Schwartzwalder, Ben (D)	Syracuse	178	96	3	0.6480	7
Shealy, Dal	Richmond	87	54	0	0.6170	17
Sherrill, Jackie	Mississippi State	175	101	4	0.6321	86
Slocum, R.C.	Texas A&M	117	41	2	0.7375	90
Snyder, Bill	Kansas State	105	49	1	0.6806	101
Solich, Frank	Nebraska	42	9	0	0.8235	44
Sparks, Ken	Carson-Newman	211	51	2	0.8030	45
Spurrier, Steve	Washington Redskins	177	59	2	0.7479	23
Stasavich, Clarence (D)	East Carolina	170	64	8	0.7190	96
Sweeney, Jim	Fresno State	196	147	4	0.5706	21
Switzer, Barry	Dallas Cowboys	202	55	8	0.7774	57
Taylor, Joe	Hampton	146	54	4	0.7255	26
Teaff, Grant	Baylor	170	150	8	0.5305	2
Tjeerdsma, Mel	Northwest Missouri	136	63	4	0.6798	91
Tomey, Dick	Arizona	158	110	4	0.5882	5
Tressel, Jim	Ohio State	142	63	2	0.6908	31
Tressel, Lee (D)	Baldwin-Wallace	155	52	6	0.7418	50
Wacker, Jim	Minnesota	160	130	3	0.5512	10
Wallace, Bobby	Temple	94	68	1	0.5798	60
Welsh, George	Virginia	190	133	4	0.5872	58
Westering, Frosty	Pacific Lutheran	294	89	7	0.7628	84
Wilkinson, Bud (D)	Oklahoma	154	49	4	0.7536	13
Wilson, Red	Duke	226	99	14	0.6873	98
Yeoman, Bill	Houston	160	108	8	0.5942	42
Young, Jim	Army	120	71	2	0.6269	61

Sports Medicine Guidelines

Dr. Fred Mueller
University of North Carolina-Chapel Hill

Dr. Fred Mueller is Professor and Chairman of the Department of Exercise and Sport Science at The University of North Carolina at Chapel Hill. He currently serves as Director of the National Center for Catastrophic Sports Injury Research at UNC and is Chairman of the American Football Coaches Association Committee on Football Injuries. He is also a member of the American College of Sports Medicine. The following are his recommendations to help reduce football injuries and make the game safer for the participants.

Medical Exam

Mandatory medical examinations and medical history should be taken before allowing an athlete to participate in football. The National Collegiate Athletic Association recommends a thorough medical examination when the athlete first enters the college athletic program and an annual health-history update with use of referral exams when warranted. If the physician or coach has any questions about the athletes' readiness to participate, the athlete should not be allowed to play. High school coaches should follow the recommendations set by their State High School Athletic Association.

Health Insurance

Each student athlete should be covered by individual, parental, or institutional medical insurance to defray the costs of significant injury or illness. At the high school level, the schools should provide information about association-provided medical insurance.

Preseason Conditioning

All personnel concerned with training football athletes should emphasize proper, gradual, and complete physical conditioning. Special emphasis should be placed on working in hot and humid weather conditions. Recommendations are as follows:

- Athletes must have a physical examination with a history of previous heat illness and type of training activities before organized practice begins.

- Acclimatize athletes to heat gradually by providing graduated practice sessions for the first 7 to 10 days and other abnormally hot or humid days.
- Know both the temperature and humidity since it is more difficult for the body to cool itself in high humidity. The use of a sling psychrometer is recommended to measure the relative humidity and anytime the wet-bulb temperature is over 78 degrees practice should be altered.
- Adjust activity levels and provide frequent rest periods. Rest in cool, shaded areas with some air movement and remove helmets and loosen or remove jerseys. Rest periods of 15 to 30 minutes should be provided during workouts of one hour.
- Provide adequate cold-water replacement during practice. *Water should always be available and in unlimited quantities to the athletes—give water regularly.*
- Salt should be replaced daily and a liberal salting of the athletes' food will accomplish this purpose. Coaches should not give salt tablets to athletes. Attention must be given to water replacement.
- Athletes should weigh each day before and after practice. Weight charts should be checked each day in order to treat athletes who lose excessive weight.
- Clothing is important and a player should avoid using long sleeves and any excess clothing. Never use rubberized clothing or sweat suits.
- Some athletes are more susceptible to heat injury than others. These individuals are not accustomed to working out in the heat, may be overweight, or may be the eager athlete who constantly competes at his capacity. Athletes with previous heat problems should be watched closely.
- It is important to observe for signs of heat illness. Some trouble signs are nausea, incoherence, fatigue, weakness, vomiting, weak rapid pulse, flushed appearance, visual disturbance, and unsteadiness. If heat illness is suspected, seek a physician's immediate service.

Facilities

It is the responsibility of the school administration to provide excellent facilities for the athletic program. The coach must monitor these facilities and keep them in the best condition.

Emergency Procedures

Each institution should strive to have a certified athletic trainer who is also a member of the school faculty. A team physician should be available for all games and readily available in other situations. There should also be a written emergency-procedure plan in place for catastrophic or serious injuries. All of the trainers and coaches should be familiar with the emergency plan.

Head and Neck Injuries

Coaches should continue to teach and emphasize the proper fundamentals of blocking and tackling to help reduce head and neck injuries. When a player has experienced or shown signs of head trauma (loss of consciousness, visual disturbances, headache, inability to walk correctly, obvious disorientation, memory loss), he should receive immediate medical attention and should not be allowed to return to practice or a game without permission from the proper medical authorities.

Records

Adequate and complete records of each injury should be kept and analyzed to determine injury patterns and to make recommendations for prevention.

Final Recommendations

- Strict enforcement of the rules of the game by both coaches and officials will help reduce injuries.
- You must keep the head out of blocking and tackling. *Keep the head out of football.*
- There should be a renewed emphasis on employing well-trained athletic personnel, providing excellent facilities, and securing the safest and best equipment available.

APPENDIX C

Medical and Legal Considerations

Dr. Herb Appenzeller
Guilford College

Dr. Herb Appenzeller is a former athletics director at Guilford College and Professor of Sports Management Emeritus. He is also a former football coach. He has authored and edited 16 books in the area of sport law, risk management, and sport management. He is the co-editor of *From The Gym To The Jury*, a sport-law newsletter. He is a member of four sports Halls of Fame. At the present, he is Executive-in-Residence in graduate Sport Administration at Appalachian State University.

No one wants an athlete to be injured. In sports activities, however, there is always the possibility of injury no matter how careful you are in observing proper procedures. And no one wants to be involved in a lawsuit. Today we have an unprecedented number of sports-related litigation that concerns everyone associated with sports.

The fact that injury occurs does not necessarily mean that the coach is negligent or liable for damages. No sure criteria exist for determining what is negligent action since each case stands individually on its own merit. The following recommendations can help prevent situations that may lead to injuries or litigation:

- Require a thorough physical examination before the athlete engages in the sport.
- Assign someone to make certain all equipment fits properly.
- Assign someone to inspect equipment for defects and the facilities for hazards. Keep an accurate record of each inspection.
- Obtain medical insurance coverage for the athlete and liability insurance for the coaches and other staff members.
- Adopt a medical plan for emergency treatment for all athletes involved in physical contact or strenuous exercise.
- Assign drills within the athlete's range of ability and commensurate with his size, skill, and physical condition.
- Prepare the athlete gradually for all physical drills and progress from simple to complex tasks in strenuous and dangerous drills.
- Warn the athlete of all possible dangers inherent in the drills in which he is involved.

- Follow the activities as designed. If the coach deviates from the prescribed drills, the decision to do so should be based on sound reasoning. Extra precautions for safety should be taken.

- Adopt a policy regarding injuries. Do not attempt to be a medical specialist in judging the physical condition of an athlete under your care.

- Require a physician's medical permission before permitting seriously injured or ill athletes to return to normal practice.

- Avoid moving the injured athlete until it is safe to do so. Whenever the athlete is moved, make certain he is taken away from potentially dangerous playing areas.

- Conduct periodic medical/legal in-service training programs for all personnel.

Risk management has become a vital part of the overall athletics program and football coaches should develop risk management strategies as they relate to their use of drills such as:

- Avoid terminology such as *suicide drills, death run, and hamburger drill*. These terms could come back to haunt you in court.

- In the event of an injury, always follow-up with a call or visit to check on the athlete's condition. However, never, never admit fault or assign blame.

- Isolate and keep under lock and key equipment involved in a serious injury (helmet, protective pads, etc.).

- Be aware that you can be sued, but don't panic. Be prepared and coach with confidence.

APPENDIX D

Summer Two-A-Day Practice Guidelines*

The American Football Coaches Association and the National Athletic Trainers' Association have launched a new educational initiative, HEAT (Helping Educate Athletes in Training). The program is designed to help coaches better prepare their athletes for the grueling conditions of two-a-day practices.

These two-a-day workouts allow for accelerated physical conditioning, increased strength training, and skill development, and can even help develop bonds between teammates. But because these workouts usually occur in hot summer months, heat-related stress becomes a serious concern. Studies have shown that football players can lose dangerously high levels of fluid in 24 hours during two-a-day workouts. Additionally, athletes who are not properly acclimatized to the heat are highly susceptible to injury.

Tips for Safer Two-A-Days

Injury rates increase during two-a-day workouts whether athletes are in peak physical condition or not. In fact, many athletes don't even make their starting lineup because of injuries incurred during preseason training. The following tips can help ensure that athletes stay at their best and prevent heat-related injuries during two-a-days.

Encourage Athletes to Begin Conditioning Before Two-A-Days

Encourage athletes to begin conditioning in the heat two weeks before official practice begins. This allows their bodies to cool more efficiently by increasing sweat production sooner than when they are not acclimated to the heat.

Avoid Workouts During Unusually Hot Temperature

Practice sessions during unusually hot and humid conditions should be limited to very moderate workouts, postponed until cooler time of the day, or brought inside to avoid the heat.

Make Fluids Part of the Playbook

Before, during, and after competition, be sure to consume adequate amounts of fluid. Athletes can make sure they are properly hydrated by checking their urine color:

*Printed with the permission of the **AFCA** and the **NATA** from their summer **HEAT** publication.*

lighter urine color indicates athletes are better hydrated. The longer the workout session, the more frequently fluids need to be replaced. Research shows that a sports drink containing a 6% carbohydrate solution, like Gatorade, can be absorbed as rapidly as water. But unlike water, a sports drink can provide energy, delay fatigue, and improve performance.

Use the Shade

Before practice, warm up in the shade and be sure to rest in the shade during breaks. Even during rest, exposure to heat can raise the body temperature, increase fluid loss, and decrease the blood available to the muscles during workouts.

Recommend Wearing Loose Fitting Clothing

Cotton blend, loose fitting clothing can help promote heat loss. The rule: the less clothing, the better.

Be Prepared for an Emergency

Always have a cell phone on hand and be familiar with emergency numbers. Also keep ice and ice towels on hand in case of heat-related emergencies.

Fluids Guidelines for Two-A-Days

Proper hydration is the best safeguard against heat illness. Remember to have athletes drink before, during, and after training and competition. The following fluid consumption guidelines can help safeguard athletes against heat-related illness.

Before Exercise

- Two to three hours before exercise drink at least 17 to 20 oz. of water or sports drink.
- Ten to twenty minutes before exercise drink another 7 to 10 oz. of water or a sports drink.

What to Drink During Exercise

- Drink early—even minimal dehydration compromises performance. In general, every 10 to 20 minutes drink at least 7 to 10 oz. of water or a sports drink. To maintain hydration remember to drink beyond thirst. Optimally, drink fluids based on amount of heat and urine loss.
- Athletes benefit in many situations from drinking a sports drink containing carbohydrate.
- If exercise lasts more than 45 to 50 minutes or is intense, a sports drink should be provided during the session.

- The carbohydrate concentration in the ideal fluid replacement solution should be in the range of 6% to 8% (14 g/ 8 oz.).
- During events when a high rate of fluid intake is necessary to sustain hydration, sport drink with less than 7% carbohydrate should be used to optimize delivery.
- Fluid with salt (sodium chloride) are beneficial to increasing thirst and voluntary fluid intake as well as offsetting the amount in lost sweat.
- Cool beverages at temperatures of 50 to 59 degrees Fahrenheit are recommended.

What Not to Drink During Exercise

- Fruit juices, carbohydrate gels, sodas, and those sports drinks that have carbohydrate levels greater than 8% area not recommended as the sole beverage.
- Beverages containing caffeine, alcohol, and carbonation are discouraged during exercises because they can dehydrate the body by stimulating excess urine production, or decrease voluntary fluid intake.

After Exercises

Immediately after training or competition is the key time to replace fluids. Weigh athletes before and after exercise. Research indicates that for every pound of weight lost, athletes should drink at least 20 oz. of fluid to optimize rehydration. Sports beverages are an excellent choice.

ABOUT THE AUTHOR

Jerry R. Tolley is the former head football coach at Elon University. Under his leadership, Elon gained a 49-11-2 record, claiming consecutive national titles in 1980 and 1981. His 1977 and 1978 squads were also nationally ranked number six and number two, respectively. During his five-year head coaching career, his teams garnered an 8-1 record in playoff bowl competition and won an impressive 80.6 % of all games played.

During his career, Tolley also received numerous coaching honors, including conference, district, state, area, and national coach of the year awards. In January 2003, he received his 35-year membership award from the American Football Coaches Association. He has also received the State of North Carolina Order of the Long Leaf Pine award and the Laurel Wreath award, the highest award given by the State of North Carolina in the area of sports and athletics.

He has written numerous football-related articles for *Coach and Athlete, The Athletic Journal, The Coaching Clinic, and the Journal of Health Physical Education, Recreation and Dance*. His doctoral dissertation was "The History of Intercollegiate Athletics for Men at Elon College."

Since his retirement from coaching, Dr. Tolley continues to serve Elon University as the director of annual giving. He is also involved in a number of community activities, having served two terms as mayor of the town of Elon, as well as serving on many local boards, including The Alamance Foundation, The Thomas E. Powell Jr. Biology Foundation, The Community Foundation of Greater Greensboro, The Alamance Education Alliance, and BEACTIVE North Carolina.

ADDITIONAL FOOTBALL RESOURCES FROM COACHES CHOICE

 Coaching Offensive Linemen (Second Edition)
Dave Christensen, University of Toledo
2003 • 248 pp • ISBN 1-58518-769-0 • $19.95

 Special Teams: The Winning Edge
Dick Arbuckle
2002 • 196 pp • ISBN 1-58518-311-3 • $18.95

 Coaching Defensive Linemen
John Levra, Buffalo Bills
1999 • 168 pp • ISBN 1-58518-212-5 • $18.95

 Coaching Offensive Backs (Second Edition)
Steve Axman, University of Washington
1997 • 216 pp • ISBN 1-58518-181-1 • $19.95

Coaching Linebackers
Jerry Sandusky, Penn State University
1995 • 136 pp • ISBN 1-58518-171-4 • $17.95

TO PLACE YOUR ORDER:

TOLL FREE: 888-229-5745
MAIL: Coaches Choice
P.O. Box 1828
Monterey, CA 93942
FAX: 831-372-6075
ONLINE: www.coacheschoice.com